THE LOS BAÑOS PRISON CAMP RAID

The Philippines 1945

GORDON L. ROTTMAN

First published in Great Britain in 2010 by Osprey Publishing,
Midland House, West Way, Botley, Oxford, OX2 0PH, UK
44–02 23rd St, Suite 219, Long Island City, NY 11101, USA
E-mail: info@ospreypublishing.com

Print ISBN: 978 1 84908 075 0
PDF e-book ISBN: 978 1 84908 076 7

Page layout by: Bounford.com, Cambridge, UK
Index by Mike Parkin
Typeset in Sabon
Maps by Bounford.com, Cambridge, UK
3D BEVs by Alan Gilliland
Originated by United Graphics Pte
Printed in China through Worldprint

10 11 12 13 14   10 9 8 7 6 5 4 3 2 1

A CIP catalog record for this book is available from the British Library

THE WOODLAND TRUST

Osprey Publishing is supporting the Woodland Trust, the UK's leading
woodland conservation charity, by funding the dedication of trees.

ACKNOWLEDGEMENTS

The author appreciates the information provided by Akira "Taki" Takizawa
and the assistance of Steve Seale. He is especially indebted to Donald
Boose, Jr, and the staff of the US Army Military History Institute. A thank
you goes to David L. Robbins, author of *Broken Jewel*, a novel of Los Baños,
for the use of present-day photographs of the Los Baños Camp area.

ABBREVIATIONS

Abn Div	Airborne Division
amtrac	amphibian tractor (LVT)
CP	command post
GFAB	Glider Field Artillery Battalion
GGC	General Guerrilla Command
GIR	Glider Infantry Regiment
HQ	Headquarters
LVT	landing vehicle, tracked (amtrac)
NCO	non-commissioned officer
PFAB	Parachute Field Artillery Battalion
PIR	Parachute Infantry Regiment
PQOG	President Quezon's Own Guerrillas
POW	prisoner of war
TCS	Troop Carrier Squadron

US ARMY OFFICER RANKS

2nd Lt	2nd Lieutenant
1st Lt	1st Lieutenant
Capt	Captain
Maj	Major
LtCol	Lieutenant Colonel
Col	Colonel
BrigGen	Brigadier General ("one-star")
MajGen	Major General ("two-star")
LtGen	Lieutenant General ("three-star")

Note: a Japanese major general equates to a US brigadier general and a
Japanese lieutenant general equates to a US major general.

MILITARY TIME

Military time using the 24-hour clock is used in this study. Military times
0001hrs to 1159hrs equate to 12.01am to 11.59am. Military times
1200hrs to 2359hrs equate to 12.00pm to 11.59pm. Subtract 12 from the
military time to determine the civilian time.

LINEAR MEASUREMENTS

Distances, ranges, and dimensions are given in the contemporary US
system of feet, yards, and statute miles rather than metric. To convert
these figures to metric the following conversion formulas are provided:

Feet to meters	multiply feet by 0.3058
Yards to meters	multiply yards by 0.9114
Miles to kilometers	multiply miles by 1.6093

CONTENTS

INTRODUCTION

In January and February 1945 two of the most successful prisoner of war (POW)/internee camp rescue raids ever conducted were executed by US Army forces fighting on Luzon in the Philippines. The Cabanatuan prison camp liberation conducted in the January by Rangers and Alamo Scouts is perhaps the better known of the two operations, being immortalized in the motion picture *The Great Raid* (2005).[1] Because of the movie Cabanatuan has overshadowed the rescue of thousands of civilian internees in a spectacular operation at Los Baños. Even at the time of the Los Baños raid it was not as widely publicized as Cabanatuan owing to another event. On the day of the Los Baños raid, February 23, 1945, a flag was raised over Iwo Jima.

Although lesser known, the Los Baños internment camp rescue was among the war's most masterfully executed raids and in many ways more spectacular than the legendary Cabanatuan raid. Los Baños was executed nearly flawlessly under difficult and challenging circumstances. The most notable among these was the extremely brief time for preparation, planning, and rehearsal time allotted to the assigned units. The Los Baños raid was a larger-scale operation involving two infantry battalions, two artillery battalions, and several smaller units as well as hundreds of Filipino guerrillas to liberate over 2,100 American and Allied civilians and evacuate them from deep within enemy-controlled territory. It was a complex airborne, amphibious, and land operation requiring precise timing by all the many elements working in concert, but separated by significant distances. In comparison, although complex and extremely dangerous, the Cabanatuan raid had involved only two Ranger companies and a guerrilla force of over 1,000 men to rescue 522 prisoners of war.

What made the Los Baños mission so crucial was that more than 2,100 civilian men, women, and children were being intentionally starved to death with their meager rations entirely halted; there was intelligence that the Japanese were possibly planning their execution, and they were too deep behind Japanese lines to await liberation by advancing American ground forces.

---

1 See Osprey Raid 3, *The Cabanatuan Prison Raid: The Philippines 1945*.

The Philippines go to war

The war struck the Philippines just hours after the Pearl Harbor attack. That assault on the US Fleet had occurred at 0300hrs, Monday December 8, Philippine time. Japanese bombers from Formosa began attacking military installations on Luzon around Manila at noon. Most American aircraft had been aloft all morning searching for approaching Japanese. They landed at Clark Air Base north of Manila before noon to refuel and were caught by 200 Japanese aircraft, which had been delayed for two hours by fog. Fewer than 60 US aircraft survived.

Although war fears were in the air, the sudden attack had stunned the 15,000 or so American civilians in the Philippines. Gen MacArthur, at the time serving as the field marshal of the fledgling Philippine Army, had not expected the Japanese to attack until at least April. Some civilians had left earlier aboard the SS *President Coolidge* in late November, and the next liner was due to leave on December 8. (This never happened.) However, despite some war fears, there was no crowd of Americans leaving the islands. It was the home of many and few could envision the ragged Japanese Army successfully invading the massive archipelago. Moreover, authorities were positive and encouraged Americans to remain. They did not want it to appear that Americans were fleeing the islands and abandoning the Filipinos.

The majority of these US citizens, 9,000, lived in and around Manila and at Baguio in northern Luzon, the Commonwealth's "summer capital," but hundreds of others were scattered throughout the Philippines' 7,000 islands. Most were on the larger islands living in the cities. Among them were government officials, engineers, miners, bankers, lawyers, technicians, administrators, businessmen, merchants, airline and shipping company representatives, teachers, clergy, nuns, missionaries, and many others, lots with their families. Some had been born and raised in the Philippines and to them the islands were home. They were on good terms with the Filipinos, although there was a definite class distinction. Most Americans did not "lord it over" the Filipinos, there being many fast and firm friendships. Of course there were Filipinos who resented Americans and their privileged position, but overall Filipinos were pro-American and the Japanese were acutely and uncomfortably aware of this.

MAY 16 1943

First internees arrive at Los Baños

Baker Memorial Hall of today's University of the Philippines at Los Baños stood just outside the camp's north corner in 1945. The camp was just to the right of the building. (Courtesy of David L. Robbins)

As softening-up continued by air attack, several diversionary landings were conducted on Luzon on December 10 and 12. The main landing, at Lingayen Gulf on Luzon's upper west coast and 130 miles north of Manila, finally came on December 22. Japanese forces were advancing on Manila from the north and south. In the meantime Manila was declared an open city in hopes of sparing its destruction and of protecting its 680,000 inhabitants. Military installations were set afire and warehouses thrown open to legalized looting; this would provide the Filipinos with needed goods and deny them to the Japanese. It was only a matter of days before it was realized that no help was coming from the United States. Uncontrolled looting, arson, and robberies spread throughout Manila. Japanese forces from the south entered the capital on January 2, 1942. American and Filipino forces conducted a fighting withdrawal and closed on Bataan Peninsula on January 6.

Thousands of American and Allied civilians were now at the mercy of their Japanese conquerors. The horrors of Nanking and other Japanese atrocities in China were well known. The day after they entered the city Japanese patrols with English-speaking officers began paying visits to the thousands of American and other foreign residents in the city. They were told to bring three days' clothing and food and informed that they were being taken to register as enemy aliens. Many were wise enough to bring money, valuables, and even dinner-ware, small appliances, books and other possessions that would prove useful when incarcerated. Many, though, were limited to two suitcases and were not told how long they would be absent.

The internees were mostly collected at Santo Tomás University in central Manila, which was to become the largest concentration. Conditions were crowded and initially confused, but sanitation facilities and food were adequate, though barely so. The Japanese attitude was moderate at this time. They even doled out a little more food in celebration of their continued victories. Bataan fell on April 9 and Corregidor on May 6.

On northern Luzon internees were held at Camp John Hays, a communications and recreation facility outside Baguio, which the Japanese had occupied on December 28. In May 1942 the internees were moved to Camp Allen inside Baguio and eventually to Santo Tomás. In the southern Philippines internees were collected at Cebu City on that island and in December 1942 they were shipped to Santo Tomás. In all there were 34 sites holding internees throughout the Philippines at one time or another. Most were small temporary sites. There were soon 4,255 internees incarcerated at Santo Tomás. As internees were brought in from other islands as many as 7,000 were held at the university. The only military personnel were 20 US Army nurses aiding the medical staff. Of these internees, 466 died in captivity and three were executed for escaping.

It was a confusing situation. Some civilians were allowed to return home to gather possessions, others were freed and did not have to return, but often were picked up months later. Some were permitted out to purchase food and services, and others when caught slipping out or returning were beaten and even executed. An Executive Committee was organized consisting of respected individuals and they dealt directly with the Japanese staff.

The internees were permitted to administer themselves so long as they complied with the numerous Japanese directives and regulations. At first the internees were expected to purchase their own food, but, with no income, what funds they had were soon running out. In July 1942 the Japanese began providing part of the food funds.

Filipinos were instrumental in aiding the internees. They donated food, mosquito netting, and other necessities, in what was known as the "package line." This proved to be an embarrassment to the Japanese as they struggled to degrade Westerners and to claim that Asians hated the defeated Americans. Subcommittees were set up to run the camp, and to provide entertainment, laundry, cooking, sanitation, garbage collection, police, medical services, schooling for the children, and even college credit courses for adults. The Committee even ran a newspaper and a jail; theft, pilfering, and malingering among internees were problems. There were movies to watch along with Japanese propaganda films and speeches about the American internment of Japanese-Americans in the States. The camp was run like a small town, although the more defiant internees often thought the Executive Committee bowed too easily to Japanese directives.The Committee was trying to balance the welfare of the internees with the intolerant and often unreasonable attitudes of their captors.

Some Americans managed to hide out with Filipino friends, but most were eventually rounded up. Initially many of those belonging to religious orders were allowed to remain free or were semi-confined to convents and schools. They were often moved from place to place and seldom allowed to minister to Filipinos. On the night of July 7, 1944, most enemy aliens remaining at large, including some 500 religious, were rounded up and sent to Los Baños.

Concerned that Allied propaganda efforts were increasing with claims of Japanese mistreatment, in March 1944 the Japanese Prisoner of War Bureau advised POW camp commanders to cease withholding Red Cross parcels and other food, clothing, and medical care from Allied POWs. Such Allied claims were undermining the Japanese war effort. However Japanese commanders responsible for internees and POWs, regardless of regulations and directives, very much did what they wanted to and for all practical purposes there was no improvement in the captives' lot.

Los Baños internment camp

To relieve overcrowding at Santo Tomás the Japanese planned to open a second internment camp at Los Baños, taking over the facilities of the Agricultural College of the Philippines. The town of Los Baños is 40 miles southeast of Manila on the southwest end of a large freshwater lake, Laguna de Bay in Laguna Province. The college grounds were 2 miles south of the fishing town. Los Baños means "the bath" in Spanish, so named because of the hot springs there. It was somewhat of a resort, with spas established.

The Japanese began construction of barracks there and asked for 800 single male volunteers initially to transfer there and complete the work. Others would join them later. Fewer than 300 volunteered, but the Japanese drew

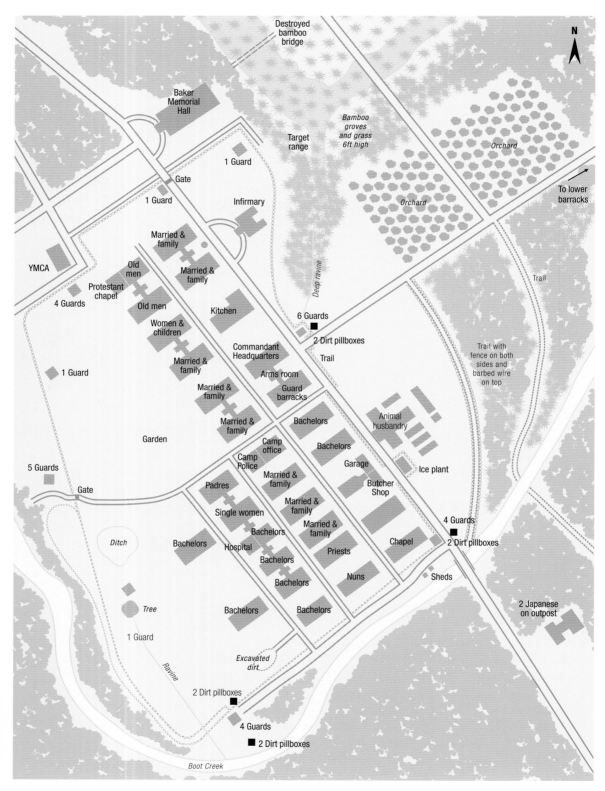

Los Baños internment camp

names of both married and single men. After a difficult railroad trip the 800 selected arrived at the uncompleted camp on May 16, 1943. The Executive Committee had opposed the move. Quarters and sanitation facilities were inadequate – there were just open pit latrines with no sewage system, the water supply was contaminated, the area's rice paddies were breeding grounds for malaria-bearing mosquitoes, and food sources were insufficient. The place was infested with bedbugs and lice. The Japanese claimed that the water, carried from far away wells, could be boiled and food cooked on wood fires. This would quickly denude the area of wood. There was no power, forcing oil lamps to be used – a serious fire hazard.

Baker Memorial Hall in May 1943, when the first group of 800 men arrived at Los Baños to help complete the camp. More were to arrive over the next year.

The Japanese ignored the problems and soon announced that Los Baños would become the main internee camp, with more moved from Santo Tomás and other sites. It was to house 7,000 people in 70 98-person barracks. One factor was that the Japanese wanted to separate the internees from their Filipino friends, who were supposed to despise their former American masters, but embarrassingly did not comply. They would be more out of the public eye in the remote area and thus would not attract continued Filipino sympathy. It would also make it more difficult for internees to escape and join the guerrillas.

In August 1943 an appeal was made to the Japanese authorities not to concentrate all the internees in such a dangerous place. The Executive Committee provided ample evidence and for once the Japanese relented and agreed that no more than 2,000 internees would be imprisoned there. Additional internees were sent from Santo Tomás: 200 in December 1943, 500 in April 1944, and 150 in December. They found the commandant to be quite reasonable; a wounded veteran of Manchuria and from an ancient samurai family, Maj Tanaka (full name unknown) was not what one would expect. He was fair, tolerant, concerned for the internees' welfare, and a Buddhist priest. Nevertheless, conditions were crowded and the internees' health was slowly deteriorating. Tanaka allowed internees to be trucked two hours to Manila to purchase food using their own, International Red Cross, and limited Japanese funds. He was replaced by Maj Urabe, who was also lenient. In July 1944, however, the new commandant arrived, Maj T. Iwanaka. His rule would be brutal. The inmates thought that he was senile and he left daily operations to the sadistic and Westerner-hating Warrant Officer Sadaaki Konishi.[2] Iwanaka did all in his means to make the internees' lives miserable after his arrival.

JULY 1944

Maj Iwanaka takes over as camp commandant

---

2 He is sometimes described as a lieutenant. Warrant officers (*jun-i*) held administrative assignments in headquarters and were treated as officers.

ORIGINS

The 100-year old dao tree, known today as the "Fertility Tree," is a landmark on the south athletic field of the University of the Philippines at Los Baños. The field beyond the tree contained barracks in 1945. (Courtesy of David L. Robbins)

MacArthur's promise of "I shall return" was well known to the residents of Los Baños and they firmly believed he would uphold his promise. It came true on September 18, 1944, when the US Sixth Army commenced the invasion of Leyte. It took almost four months to secure the island, which was far to the south of Luzon. Mindoro, closer to Luzon, was assaulted on December 15. The internees began seeing air battles high overhead and bomber formations from the south frequently roared over en route to Manila and other targets north. Filipinos smuggled in news along with food and

medicine and the internees had secreted away a few clandestine radios. The big day came on January 9, 1945, when the Sixth Army landed in Lingayen Gulf. The American landing site was some 160 miles north of Los Baños with numerous Japanese on the intervening terrain as well as in Manila. It was anyone's guess how long it would take for their deliverance to arrive. No one expected it to arrive on the wings of angels.

The closer to Manila the US I and XIV corps fought, the stiffer was the Japanese resistance. The situation was becoming desperate. Warrant Officer Konishi increasingly denied the internees food and medicine. There were growing fears they might be relocated or worse.

As the Sixth Army approached Manila, MacArthur grew increasingly alarmed over the plight of the internees and the few remaining POWs – most had been shipped to Japan and occupied territories as slave labor. The Cabanatuan prison camp raid was ordered on January 26 and successfully carried out on the night of the 30th. It was highly successful and US casualties among the raiders and POWs were negligible. The Japanese suffered heavily.

The next rescue operation would liberate the internees at Santo Tomás; it was ordered the day after Cabanatuan was liberated, January 31. Gen MacArthur visited the 1st Cavalry Division and gave MajGen Verne D. Mudge a set of simple instructions: "Go to Manila. Go around the Nips, bounce off the Nips, but go to Manila. Free the internees at Santo Tomás." Mudge assigned the mission to his 1st Cavalry Brigade and BrigGen William C. Chase organized a "flying column" using all available vehicles with troopers riding on tanks. They would make a cavalry-like lightning-fast strike into the heart of Manila 100 miles to the south, dashing out ahead of the rest of the division.[3] The 11th Airborne Division (11th Abn Div) landed at Nasugary 55 miles south of Manila the next day.

The flying column departed in the first hour of February 1, moving on three different roads toward Cabanatuan 20 miles to the southeast. The rest of the 1st Cavalry Brigade followed. The rapid advance allowed some bridges to be captured intact.

The flying column punched through the outer defenses and the road was clear to Manila. At times the column would speed forward, but destroyed bridges and roadblocks would briefly halt it. All bridges over the Angat River were destroyed, but the cavalrymen discovered a ford. The aim was to avoid decisive engagements and thrust into Manila to rescue the 3,700 US, British, Australian, Canadian, Dutch, and other nationality internees at Santo Tomás University. The flying column raced across the city limits at 1835hrs on February 3, making it the first US force to enter Manila. At 2050hrs they reached the university guided by guerrillas. They had covered 100 miles in 66 hours.

After a brief skirmish US troops reached Santo Tomás. The Japanese guards forced 200 internees into a building and threatened to kill them. The Americans negotiated their release, promising the Japanese safe passage

---

3 See Osprey Elite 175, *World War II US Cavalry Units: Pacific Theater.*

SEPTEMBER 18 1944

US Sixth Army commences invasion of Leyte

JANUARY 9 1945

US Sixth Army lands in Lingayen Gulf

to a point near Malacañan Palace (Philippine "White House"). The guards were escorted there on the 5th with only their personal weapons. Unbeknownst to them the palace had been occupied by the Americans. The escorting Americans and Japanese saluted one another and went their separate ways, but some of the guards were later killed as they moved to the palace. The survivors soon found themselves back at Santo Tomás as prisoners.

The 3,700 internees were in pathetic condition, but there was no food available other than what little the cavalrymen had. The Catholic bishop was able to collect sufficient food, while XIV Corps sent in a field hospital to care for the liberated internees. Just blocks away, a 148th Infantry Regiment, 37th Infantry Division patrol reached the Old Bilibid Prison[4] near the dockyards and discovered over 1,200 American POWs and internees abandoned by the Japanese. The vicious battle for Manila would last until March 3, when Japanese resistance finally ceased. Over 100,000 Filipino civilians were killed in the fighting, with most murdered by the Japanese.

Now of major concern were the 2,130 internees at Los Baños 30 miles south of Manila. Defending Manila were 16,000 troops under Admiral Iwabuchi Sanji, the Manila Naval Defense Force. There were also Imperial Army elements of the Shimbu Group defending the southern portion of the city. Most of the Shimbu Group, built around the 8th Division, was further south and responsible for the defense of southern Luzon, the rugged Picol Peninsula that jutted 200 miles to the southeast from the island's main mass.

---

[4] This was the old national prison dating from 1865 and now serving as the Manila City Jail, as well as housing POWs and internees. It is not to be confused with the New Bilibid Prison, opened in 1940 in southeast Manila near the shores of Laguna de Bay, where the rescued Los Baños internees would be taken.

INITIAL STRATEGY

To take pressure off I and XIV corps fighting into Manila from the north, to attack the city from another direction, and to cut the city off from reinforcement by the Shimbu Group, the 11th Abn Div would conduct an amphibious and airborne assault at Nasugbu Bay just south of Manila Bay and 55 miles southwest of the city.

The landing at Nasugbu – Operation *Mike VI* – was planned for January 31, 1945, X-Day. Initially only a single regiment, 188th Glider Infantry Regiment (188th GIR), would land as a reconnaissance-in-force. If resistance was light, the rest of the division would come ashore. The 187th GIR would be in reserve to land on order. The 511th Parachute Infantry Regiment (511th PIR) was moved to Mindoro by sea and air to stage at San José for its part of the operation. It would parachute onto Tagaytay Ridge 20 miles east of Nasugbu to secure Highway 17, which ran east then north to Manila. The 511th would be delivered in three waves on January 2–3, so long as it was felt the division could reach the ridge within 24 hours after the drop.

The convoy departed Leyte on the 27th to arrive off Nasugbu at dawn on the 31st. 1/188th GIR went ashore on Beach Red experiencing light fire. The battalion pushed inland as 2/188th landed to clear flanking enemy positions. In the afternoon 1/187th was sent ashore and attached to the 188th, followed by 2/187th. The 188th pressed inland on Highway 17 toward Tagaytay Ridge. The ridge's west end was reached after midnight, but increasing resistance slowed the advance. The delay caused the jump to be rescheduled for January 3–4. The Reconnaissance Platoon followed a trail north of the highway to determine enemy strength. Infiltrating over another trail, the 511th's demolition platoon made its way to the ridge to mark the drop zone (DZ). On the morning of February 3, the 188th attacked eastward up Highway 17 following the crest of the 8-mile-long Tagaytay Ridge. The 511th would parachute on to the ridge near its west end and attack westward to trap the Japanese rear holding up the 188th. The 2,000 x 4,000-yard DZ was mostly cultivated fields. Coordination with guerrillas had cleared out most Japanese.

Only 48 C-47s were available, a third of what was needed to deliver the regiment in one lift. The 1st Battalion boarded its transports at San José on the south end of Mindoro, some 150 miles to the south of the DZ. Approaching from the south at 0815hrs, the 1st Battalion jumped onto the ridge marked by the pathfinders. The 2nd Battalion was dropped 8,000 yards east-northeast of the DZ and further along the ridge because of the premature release of external bundles from one aircraft. The third lift with 3rd Battalion dropped at 1210hrs. Eighty men landed on the DZ, but the following aircraft saw the grounded parachutes of the second mis-dropped lift and dropped in the same place. The regiment was able to assemble in five hours. The 511th linked up with the 188th at 1300hrs. The 457th Parachute Field Artillery Battalion (PFAB) and supporting elements were dropped the next morning. A probable total of 1,830 men jumped (sources are in conflict, with some stating 1,750).

With the mid-afternoon arrival of 21/2-ton trucks from the beach, 2/511th boarded and headed for Manila. The Reconnaissance Platoon and guerrillas reported the route clear, the latter having made it so. The trucks began shuttling troops north. By midnight of the 4th, the lead elements were on the southern outskirts of Manila.

Halted at Parañaque, the division now faced the well-developed Genko Line, an in-depth position with 1,200 pillboxes backed by over 40 artillery pieces, scores of light antiaircraft guns in the ground-fire role, and over 300 machine-guns on the south side of Manila, stretching from Nichols Field on Manila Bay inland to Ft William McKinley and tied into Laguna de Bay – a 5 mile-wide front. The 511th was on the left with 2/187th attached and the 188th on the right with 1/187th attached. The division attacked into the Japanese positions. Fighting was vicious and it was almost three weeks before the division fought through. It took from February 7–12 to capture Nichols. Contact was made with 1st Cavalry Division patrols from the north on the 11th. To clear the shore of Laguna de Bay, a task force under the assistant division commander was formed on February 14. It took from the 18th–23rd to clear the area.

Having taken Nichols, the rest of the division attacked northeast to seize Ft McKinley, requiring the 13th–19th to secure it. Cavite Naval Ammunition Depot on Manila Bay was secured on the 21st. The Los Baños raid would be executed on the 23rd.

The situation in Los Baños

The weary and starving inmates of Los Baños received a New Year's gift on the final day of 1944, when US Navy fighters over-flew the camp. More aircraft were seen in the following days. The inmates were heartened, but not permitted to demonstrate any elation. They could barely contain themselves on January 6 when columns of smoke showed that the Japanese were burning their records. Even more astounding was that the next morning the camp's administration was formally turned over to the Executive Committee. The guards marched off after collecting all the picks and shovels. American and British flags were hoisted and national anthems

Inmates of the Los Baños internment camp managed as best they could for three long years of captivity. Here they make do with outdoor washing facilities.

sung. Storerooms were opened and for once sufficient food was issued. The internees also purchased food from local Filipinos on Red Cross credit (which was repaid after the war). A *Kempeitai* military police guard arrived later in the morning to secure the front gate, but did not interfere with the inmates. The Americans landed north of Manila on January 9, 1945, elating the inmates even more.

The inmates wisely chose to remain in the camp. There was no place to go, no means of transportation, and they were still weak. It was decided they should stay at the camp as US troops might arrive at any time. In addition, there were Japanese troops and *Makapili*[5] infesting the area. An air attack on nearby Japanese installations, improved food, and their freedom from guards increased the prisoners' morale and optimism.

On January 14 "Freedom Week" was over. The guards returned early that morning, filthy, exhausted, and fewer in number. Some think the guards believed they were fleeing to safety, but had suffered air attacks. Some appeared to have deserted or may have been reassigned. The prevalent theory is that they dug fortifications in Manila, perhaps on the Genko Line. They were actually safer at the camp, for now, as it would not be attacked by US aircraft and artillery.

Maj Iwanaka immediately clamped down on the internees, severely cut rations, increased roll calls and surprise searches, and enacted a shoot-on-sight curfew from 0700–1900hrs rather than at 2200hrs. Many felt that the

---

5 Pro-Japanese Filipino collaborators, *Kalipunang Makabayan ng mga Pilipino* – Patriotic League of Filipinos.

guards were on edge because of the US landing and that they had suffered from loss of face by leaving the camp. American aircraft disappeared for days and the hoped-for departure of the guards never occurred. Rations were cut so severely that the inmates were starving. Fears increased as to what would become of them. Certain food supplies were exhausted and no supplies were delivered. Illness and disease increased and one or two inmates were dying daily. The Japanese began digging holes, claiming they were foundations for new buildings – at this late date? They may have been air raid slit trenches or mass graves. Two internees on food forays returning to camp were shot on different nights.

In the early days the inmates had been able to buy bananas, camotes, coconuts, mangos, and papayas to supplement their main food, rice. Carabao (water buffalo) and pork were scarce, but obtainable. Meat was usually served in stews. From late 1944 rations were at starvation level, about 900 calories a day. Inmates were receiving a handful (81/2–101/2oz) of *palay* (unhusked rice), which had to be painstakingly husked before cooking into a mush called *lugau* complete with weevils and other bugs for protein. They also cooked weeds and banana stalks.

The rescue planners' best information was that there were 2,130 inmates. Twelve Navy nurses were the only military personnel. It was estimated that at least 50 percent were in seriously weakened condition (it was higher) and that some 250 were bedridden. A large percentage were elderly, women, and small children. It was known that most, even those in better shape, did not have the stamina for a lengthy foot march.

These *bancas* on Laguna de Bay today are no different from the boats used to transport Reconnaissance Platoon scouts and guerrillas across the lake to the Los Baños area 65 years earlier. These approximately 20ft-long boats could carry 6–8 passengers. (Courtesy of David L. Robbins)

Some bold inmates snuck out of the camp at night to find food and news. They had little luck with food, but the news was heartening. The Americans were fighting through Manila and winning. The glow of artillery flashes and fires could be seen over the horizon. One of these men, Freddy Zervoulakos, linked up with guerrilla Col Ingles on February 12 when he was conducting his reconnaissance (see below). Zervoulakos, after providing Ingles with valuable information, returned to the camp and reported to the Executive Committee. They now knew something was afoot. The cautious Committee decided that further contact with the guerrillas could be dangerous. Others felt differently and Zervoulakos and George Gray met with Ingles again, but they too became concerned with Ingles' proposals. He first suggested that arms be smuggled into the camp so that the internees could defend themselves. This was in violation of international law (Gray had been a lawyer on the US High Commission), and the prisoners would be no match for the guards. They also feared the idea of guerrillas attacking guard posts, certain that all the guards could not be wiped out and afraid that an attack would quickly result in retaliation. They emphasized to Ingles that most of the inmates were too sick and weak to walk any distance. Gray urged Ingles not to take any unilateral action without the approval of the US command.

Making it back to the camp, they again reported to the Committee what they had learned. The Committee decreed no further contact with Ingles. However Gray felt it was essential to keep communications open so that inmates were aware of what was transpiring. Zervoulakos, Ben Edwards, and Pete Miles crept out of the camp on February 18. They contacted the guerrillas at a pre-arranged point and hoped to make it to US lines to inform them of their plight. Guerrillas transported Miles by *banca* across the lake, while the other two remained in Nanhaya being debriefed by guerrillas.

A *banca* is a traditional Filipino canoe used for fishing and short distance transportation on lakes and coastal waters. They are proportionally long with a very narrow beam and sharply pointed bow. Smaller boats are about 20ft, but larger ones were built. A 20ft-plus boat could carry six to eight people. They typically have two short masts serving a dual purpose: to anchor guy lines to support the outriggers on both sides and to hold a horizontal pole between them for a sun/rain canopy. Most are propelled by paddles, but a taller mast could be rigged and a sail used. Even larger motorized inter-island *bancas* were used. *Bancas* were designed to be run up onto the beach where no piers are available.

The guerrillas successfully performed the lake crossing, and got Miles to the 11th Abn Div command post (CP) before noon the next day. Miles provided the division staff with extremely valuable information, including not only the locations of guard posts and machine-guns, but also their fields of fire. Many were camouflaged and not detectable on aerial photos. Most of the guns were sited to fire on escaping inmates and were not set up for perimeter defense. The main gate gun only covered the road and could not be traversed to cover the approaches across the fields. The guards' routine and their posts were critical – in fact, the most important information was the guards' morning routine. At 0645hrs the off-duty guards and staff fell in for calisthenics in an open field beside their barracks. They conducted 30 minutes of *radyo taisho* broadcast over Radio Manila – until it went off the air. They wore only loincloths and their rifles were locked in the arms room that linked the commandant's headquarters and their barracks. Only the guards standing post were armed. However, it was not known whether the next shift of guards was armed and ready to relieve the duty guards; if so, some 40–50 armed guards would be present. This information on the guards' routine was not only of obvious benefit to the attackers; it would also help protect the inmates from vengeful guards.

Events began to move quickly now. On February 20 the divisional Reconnaissance Platoon leader and an engineer platoon leader arrived from across the lake and linked up with the guerrillas and two Americans at Nanhaya. The two lieutenants were to reconnoiter the camp's defenses, locate guard posts, select a DZ, plot a route from the DZ to the camp, select a landing beach and find a route to the camp. In this the guerrillas assisted, as did the two internees. They conducted a close reconnaissance, accomplishing all tasks.

The 1,500 x 3,200ft DZ they selected was on the northeast side of the camp. Several dry stream beds and gullies ran across it, providing cover as the paratroopers rushed toward the camp. Depending on where a paratrooper landed, it could be only a few hundred feet to several hundred yards to the camp. The length of its northeast side was edged with a railroad track and a power line crossed the north corner (power had been cut). To the south of the camp was a possible DZ, but water-filled Boot Creek lay between it and the camp. The two officers returned to the division CP by *banca* on the 21st. The planning staff and the units conducting the raid now possessed highly detailed information from several reliable sources.

The 11th Airborne Division

The 11th Abn Div was the third of the five US airborne divisions activated.[6] This division was unique in that it was the only one to be deployed to the Pacific.[7] The life of "The Angels" began on February 25, 1943 at Camp Mackall, North Carolina, the home of the Airborne Command. The division was assigned a parachute infantry regiment, the 511th, and two glider infantry regiments, 187th and 188th. To better understand the division's organization, it must be understood that the parachute regiment had three battalions and the glider regiments only two. The parachute artillery battalion had four four-howitzer batteries (unique for the 457th) and the glider battalions had two six-howitzer batteries.

The 511th PIR had been activated earlier, on January 5, at Camp Toccoa, Georgia, and moved to Camp Mackall just before the division's activation. The division's units underwent basic training that ran through the summer

The 11th Airborne Division, "The Angels," was assigned to plan and execute the Los Baños raid in February 1945. The only airborne division to fight in the Pacific, it had fought on Leyte and Luzon before being assigned the rescue mission.

---

6 See Osprey Battle Orders 26, *US Airborne Units in the Pacific Theater 1942–45.*
7 There was one other airborne unit in the Pacific, the 503rd PIR, which was separate from the 11th Abn Div and maintained for special missions. It was the 503rd that jumped at Nadzab, New Guinea; Noemfoor Island, and Corregidor Island.

AMERICAN PARATROOPER

A typical paratrooper rifleman was armed with a .30cal Garand M1 rifle and at least two Mk II fragmentation grenades. They traveled light with D- and K-rations stuffed in pockets. Their only equipment was a cartridge belt with 80 rounds of clipped ammunition, a first aid pouch, and canteen. A poncho was folded and tied to the back of their cartridge belt. No packs were carried.

11TH AIRBORNE DIVISION, FEBRUARY 1945

- HQ, 11th Airborne Division (11th Abn Div)
- HQ Company, 11th Abn Div
- 187th Glider Infantry Regiment (187th GIR)
- 188th Glider Infantry Regiment (188th GIR)
- 511th Parachute Infantry Regiment (511th PIR)
- 127th Airborne Engineer Battalion
- 152nd Airborne Antiaircraft Artillery Battalion
- 11th Abn Div Artillery
  - HQ & HQ Battery
  - 457th Parachute Field Artillery Battalion
  - 674th Glider Field Artillery Battalion
  - 675th Glider Field Artillery Battalion
- Special Troops
  - 221st Airborne Medical Company
  - 408th Airborne Quartermaster Company
  - 511th Airborne Signal Company
  - 711th Airborne Ordnance Maintenance Company
  - Military Police Platoon, 11th Abn Div
  - Provisional Parachute Maintenance Company, 11th Abn Div
  - Provisional Reconnaissance Platoon, 11th Abn Div
  - Counterintelligence Corps Detachment, 11th Abn Div
  - Language Detachment, 11th Abn Div

Attachments on Luzon

19th Infantry Regiment, 24th Infantry Division
472nd Field Artillery Battalion (105mm Howitzer, Tractor-Drawn)
Company A, 44th Tank Battalion (M4 tank)
Company B, 637th Tank Destroyer Battalion (M18 TD)
Company C, Boat Battalion, 532nd Engineer Boat & Shore Regiment
Battery D, 102nd AAA Automatic Weapons Battalion (40mm/.50 cal)
Cannon Company, 21st Infantry Regiment, 24th Infantry Division (105mm M7 SP)
5th & 7th Medical Portable Surgical Hospitals
407th Medical Collecting Company, Separate
1st Platoon, 605th Medical Clearing Company, Separate

when unit training began in June. In May and June, after completing basic training, the parachute units traveled to Ft Benning, Georgia and undertook parachute training.[8] In December 1943, with much debate underway regarding the retention of airborne divisions, the 11th Abn Div took part in the Knollwood Maneuvers. The exercise was successful and convinced officials that airborne divisions should be retained.

In January 1944 the 11th Abn Div relocated to Camp Polk, Louisiana, where it undertook additional unit training and testing. In April the division

---

[8] Only the 511th PIR, 457th PFAB, an engineer company, and other minor elements of the 11th Abn Div were parachute-qualified. All other units were delivered by gliders and transports.

arrived at Camp Stoneman, California, for overseas deployment. It was assembled in New Guinea by May and began jungle training and later undertook amphibious assault training. During this time the unit operated a jump school to train many of the glider troops as paratroopers and expand the division's capabilities.

The division departed for Leyte in October to arrive in November, after the main Sixth Army landing had taken place in the first phase of the liberation of the Philippines. There the division fought a vicious 58-day battle in central Leyte's jungle-covered mountains, enduring rain, mud, disease, Japanese infiltrations, even a Japanese parachute assault, and facing an almost impossible supply situation. The 11th suffered over 500 casualties and also lost many to disease, fatigue, and injuries. Nevertheless, although the campaign was grueling, the division had gained a great deal of combat experience on rugged terrain under harsh conditions that would serve it well in its coming actions. It had proved extremely flexible, made do with limited resources, developed a high degree of teamwork, and demonstrated a great deal of innovation. These qualities were to be of great value to the division, and especially to the units selected for the Los Baños raid.

A month after operations had been completed on Leyte, the 11th Abn Div conducted an amphibious and airborne assault on Luzon. Only a smattering of replacements had been received. This was well to the south of Manila, and just under three weeks after the main US landing further to the north of Manila on January 9 described earlier.

Such was the state of the 11th Abn Div when its elements conducted the Los Baños raid. It had conducted an exhausting two-month jungle and mountain battle on Leyte and then had fought for another brutal month in jungle conditions, assaulting through strongly fortified positions. It had suffered over 1,500 combat casualties and lost many men through illness, exhaustion, and non-battle injuries, most of whom were in the infantry battalions. Some rifle companies, authorized 127 men, were down to 50 effectives. The division still had over two hard months of campaigning ahead to clear southern Luzon. No replacements would be received until after the campaign.

THE PLAN

To clarify command and control, the 11th Abn Div had been under LtGen Robert L. Eichelberger's Eighth Army control when it landed at Nasugbu on January 31, 1945. While fighting through the Gecko Line, it was transferred to LtGen Walther Kruger's Sixth Army control on February 9 and the next day to MajGen Oscar W. Griswold's XIV Corps. Neither of these headquarters would have any meaningful role in planning the rescue.

The Eighth Army tasked the 11th Abn Div with the mission on February 3, but it was not able to commence the operation at that point. The division had just reached Tagaytay Ridge and the 511th PIR was jumping in to reinforce the glider regiments advancing on the ground. The division still had a long and hard fight ahead of it. Los Baños was 20 miles to the east of where it was then fighting and over 40 miles south of where it would fight through the Genko Line. Nonetheless, the division staff, even while preoccupied with a brutal fight, collected intelligence and undertook tentative planning. By the 15th, a picture of the situation at Los Baños was emerging from aerial photos and information supplied by guerrillas. The target date was set for February 23, a moonless night, critical for the amtracs crossing the lake. Even a partial moon casts a beam of light on a water's surface straight back to the observer, be he ashore or aboard a moving patrol boat. Anything crossing the swatch of reflected moonlight will be silhouetted.

It was recognized that two battalions were needed for this operation, one to cross the lake aboard amphibious vehicles, secure the beachhead, move to the camp to reinforce the parachute-delivered rescue force, and aid in evacuating the camp and protecting the internees as they withdrew to the beachhead or moved to link up with the diversionary force. The other battalion was required to provide this overland diversionary force thrusting from the west.

A full battalion was unnecessary for the lake-crossing battalion as Japanese strength in the immediate area was known to be light. Additionally, as much space as possible was necessary in the amphibious vehicles for the freed internees. A key component of the operation was a parachute company,

and since the parachute company and the amphibious-delivered battalion would link up it made sense that the former be organic to the latter. The diversionary battalion could be selected from any regiment.

It would be a strain on the division, which was already significantly smaller than an infantry division, to have to pull two infantry battalions out of the line along with supporting artillery. There was still a week and half of fighting before Manila was secured, and at the time it was not known how much longer the battle might continue. It was hoped the units could return to normal operations within 24 hours after the raid. The 503rd PIR, a separate unit not assigned to the 11th Abn Div, though unengaged in early February was nonetheless unavailable. It was being readied for the February 16 jump onto Corregidor and would be engaged there until March 8.

It was not practical to employ the 6th Ranger Battalion that had so successfully executed the Cabanatuan raid. The 11th Abn Div and the Ranger battalion were both assigned to Sixth Army, but the Ranger battalion's companies were scattered north of Manila conducting reconnaissance patrols and economy-of-force operations. The unit would have to be moved through embattled Manila and not being organic to the 11th Abn Div it would have been difficult to integrate it into the division's multi-phased operation. The Alamo Scouts, who had so successfully supported the Cabanatuan raid, were also unavailable. Their small teams were scattered all over Luzon assisting and providing liaison with guerrilla units.

MajGen. Joseph M. Swing, Commanding General, 11th Airborne Division, relied on his subordinate commanders to develop and execute an effective plan. Swing and the accompanying officer wear the "Swing cap," made in both olive drab and khaki in Australia.

FEBRUARY 3 1945

11th Airborne Division tasked with mission

The 511th PIR was organized into a headquarters and headquarters company with a service company, medical detachment, and three infantry battalions. The battalions included a headquarters and headquarters company, medical detachment, and three rifle companies. Within the battalion headquarters company were a mortar platoon (with four 81mm M1s) and a light machine-gun platoon (with eight .30cal M1919A4s). The regimental headquarters company possessed a demolition platoon with a section for attachment to each battalion.

The 127-man rifle company had a headquarters and three rifle platoons. A platoon's two 12-man rifle squads each had an M1919A4 light machine-gun (LMG). The platoon also had a seven-man headquarters and a six-man 60mm M2 mortar squad. Parachute rifle squads were not normally issued .30cal M1918A2 Browning automatic rifles (BAR), but the 11th Abn Div often used them in lieu of the machine-guns. Most troops carried .30cal M1 Garand rifles. There were few .30cal M1 carbines and even fewer .45cal M1928A1 Thompson submachine guns; authorized one per squad. Some men carried the new .45cal M3 "grease guns." In theory every paratrooper was additionally armed with a .45cal M1911A1 Colt pistol, but many did not carry them. Platoons usually carried a 2.36in M9 bazooka.

Company B, 1st Battalion, 511th PIR was under the command of 1st Lt John M. Ringler. While it was proud to be selected for the mission, the reality was that the company was chosen not because of any particular reputation, notable tactical skills, or dynamic leadership. The decision was more pragmatic. With an effective strength of 93 men, it had the highest strength of any of the rifle companies, at 73 percent. In fact the 1st Battalion was selected because it had the highest strength of the 511th's three battalions, 412 as opposed to the authorized 530. To reinforce the understrength company it was beefed up with the battalion light machine-gun platoon. This platoon was authorized 42 men and eight LMGs, but its actual strength was 28 men, probably with four to six LMGs. At the last minute a nine-man engineer squad (only two men short) with its platoon leader was added to prepare roadblocks. This totaled 130 paratroopers, but it is known that at least one war correspondent and three Filipino volunteers also jumped.

The Provisional Reconnaissance Platoon, 11th Abn Div, had been formed in the fall of 1943 when the division was at Camp Mackall. Airborne divisions lacked the company-size reconnaissance troop assigned to infantry divisions. Most formed a reconnaissance platoon from handpicked men. The division G-2 Section under Maj Henry Muller, who later planned the Los Baños mission, put out a call for volunteers. The original platoon leader, 1st Lt Jim Polka, did not limit himself to selecting infantrymen. He sought men with a variety of skills that would prove useful, including engineers with demolitions experience, artillerymen who could adjust fire, radio operators, and medics. One NCO was a Filipino and spoke Tagalog. Thirty-five men were selected from 300 volunteers. Any not parachute-qualified undertook the training. They had to be able to operate independently, but teamwork was essential. A large percentage were college students with athletic and outdoors experience. They had to be smart, flexible, and adaptable. Training included individual and small unit tactics, scouting, land navigation, camouflage, intelligence collecting and reporting, first aid, weapons, demolitions, communications, survival, rubber boat handling, hand-to-hand combat, physical fitness, organized athletics, and more. The platoon's training continued in Australia and New Guinea where some members attended the Australian Canangra Jungle Warfare School and the Alamo Scouts Training Center. It was not long before the freewheeling unit became known as the "Ghost Platoon" or "Killer Platoon."

The platoon answered to MajGen Swing and the G-2, Muller. Swing wanted a small special unit under his immediate control able to respond instantly to mission requirements. He did not want to wait for subordinate staffs to detail a unit that might or might not have met his needs. As it was a provisional unit with men detached on paper from their parent units, promotions were frozen and all equipment had to be obtained by whatever means necessary. On Leyte Lt Polka was promoted out of the platoon; 1st Lt George E. Skau took command and would remain there until his death in an aircraft crash on Okinawa at the war's end.

A critical unit was the 672nd Amphibian Tractor Battalion. It had been raised as the 672nd Tank Destroyer Battalion (Self-Propelled) on June 19, 1943 at Camp Hood, Texas. The need for tank destroyers had been reassessed and they began to be reduced in number. On April 15, 1944, it was

ALAMO SCOUTS TRAINING CENTER

In November 1943 LtGen Kruger commanding Sixth Army in the Southwest Pacific Area directed the formation of a special reconnaissance unit. Kruger desired a dedicated unit that was not only able to collect coastal intelligence for landing operations, but could penetrate inland.

On November 21 LtCol Fredrick W. Bradshaw of the Sixth Army G-2 Section was directed to establish the Alamo Scouts Training Center (ASTC). It was opened on Fergusson Island 40 miles off the southeast end of New Guinea in December. The Center borrowed training concepts from the Navy's Special Service Unit #1 (an amphibious reconnaissance unit) and Scout and Raider School in Florida, Army Rangers, and Australian commandos. The grueling six-week course included physical conditioning, hand-to-hand combat, jungle survival, basic native languages and customs, intelligence collection, scouting and patrolling, camouflage, navigation, communications, Allied and enemy weapons, infiltration and exfiltration techniques, and rubber boats. The course also taught the importance of patience and stealth.

Candidates were selected from Sixth Army combat units through a series of interviews and were required to have combat experience, be able to swim, be in excellent physical condition, and possess 20/20 vision. Class size was about 35 with up to 40 percent attrition.

Most graduates were returned to their units to serve as scouts and impart their skills. Fewer than half of the 250 enlisted graduates and a third of the 75 officers were retained to serve in the Alamo Scouts, formerly designated the Sixth Army Special Reconnaissance Unit.

Six members of the 11th Abn Div's Scout Platoon attended ASTC Class 4 conducted at Mange Point, Finschhafen, New Guinea in April 1944. All graduated with the exception of one who came down with dengue fever. One was selected for retention by the Alamo Scouts and another was reassigned to the 511th PIR's Intelligence and Reconnaissance Platoon. Three men returned to the Reconnaissance Platoon to pass on their skills, which proved to be of great value.

LVT(4) AMPHIBIAN TRACTOR

The 672nd Amphibian Tractor Battalion was equipped with landing vehicles, tracked Mk IV built by the Food Machinery Corporation at Dunedin, Florida. Although the fourth variant of the amtrac, the LVT(4) was actually the third to be fielded. (The LVT(3), actually a better vehicle which became the post-war standard, was not fielded until later owing to production delays.) The LVT(4) had seen its first combat employment at Saipan the previous June by the Marines. It had since been widely used to support amphibious landings in the Philippines. The full-tracked vehicle weighed 14 tons with a length of 24ft. It was basically a tracked box with the three-man crew (tractor commander, driver, assistant driver/radio operator), 250hp gasoline engine, SCR-528 radio, and .50cal M2 and .30cal M1917A1 machine-guns forward. Most amtracs of the 672nd mounted only a single .50cal, although some did have two. An amtrac crew was also armed with a .45cal Thompson M1 submachine gun and two .30cal M1 carbines.

The vehicle could carry 8,000lb of cargo including a jeep or 105mm howitzer, or 24 combat-equipped troops. It was the first LVT fielded with a rear cargo ramp and this was of great benefit when loading and unloading the weakened internees. The LVT(4) had a range of 150 miles on land reaching up to 20mph, and 75 miles on water with a top speed of 71/2mph. Cargo LVTs were not armored fighting vehicles. They were protected only by thin non-hardened sheet steel, not armor. They were slow and high-profiled, making the large vehicles easy targets. Their low ground clearance made them susceptible to high-centering on rocks, stumps, and rough ground as well as being prone to mechanical breakdown. Their bilge pump had to run continuously. If the engine quit while afloat the vehicle would soon flood and sink. Regardless of the vehicle's flaws, one of the key factors contributing to the success of the Los Baños raid was the amtracs and their remarkable abilities.

redesignated an amtrac battalion at Ft Ord, California. It departed for the Pacific in September 1944, served on Bougainville, and then supported the Luzon landing on January 9, 1945. On February 7 it transported assault elements of the 37th Infantry Division across the Pasig River inside Manila. In July 1945 it landed Australian troops on Borneo. It returned to the United States at the end of 1945 and was deactivated.

A 502-man amtrac battalion consisted of a 93-man headquarters, headquarters and service company, a 12-man medical detachment, and two 194-man amtrac companies. Each company had 51 LVTs organized into a headquarters platoon with three LVTs and three tractor platoons each with 16 LVTs – one in the headquarters and five in each of the three sections.

The original plan called for the use of DUKW ("Duck") amphibious trucks as the vehicle of choice. It is not known why they were replaced by amtracs. The Ducks would have performed better on roads, but tracked amtracs would be better for cross-country travel and busting through barbed wire fences and gates. It could be that Ducks were needed for ship-to-shore transfer of supplies, for which they were in high demand. Both the Duck and the amtrac carried 24 passengers; but the amtrac with its deep cargo compartment and 8,000lb cargo capacity could better handle an overload of passengers than the Duck with a 4,000lb capacity. While amtracs were unarmored, their steel bodies were heavier than the Ducks' and would provide slightly more protection. Additionally each amtrac had one or two .50cal machine-guns while only one in four Ducks mounted a .50cal. The use of amtracs was a calculated risk as they had a startlingly high mechanical failure rate, and they would be pushed hard on this operation.

Command and control of the Los Baños mission was conducted very differently than in the previous month's Cabanatuan raid. That operation had been directly planned and coordinated by Sixth Army with direct control over the 6th Ranger Battalion and with the guerrilla units under central command cooperating directly with the Rangers.

For Los Baños, Sixth Army tasked the 11th Abn Div to plan and execute the mission using its own and some attached resources. The multiple guerrilla units were coordinated through the General Guerrilla Command (GGC) headquarters, which exercised a varying degree of control over the disparate units. Since XIV Corps and Sixth Army were not involved in the planning, the first hint that XIV Corps had of how the mission would be conducted was when the division requested the use of amtracs on February 19. Sixth Army did not find out until the day before the raid was launched.

Sixth Army tasked the 11th Abn Div with the mission on February 5 and Gen Swing immediately directed the G-2, LtCol Henry "Butch" Muller, to begin collecting intelligence on Los Baños. The G-3, Col Douglass P. "Doug" Quandt, was told to develop a plan to rescue the over 2,100 inmates – go in, free them, and bring them out. The division CP was at Parañaque on the shores of Manila Bay, south of the embattled city.

Several intelligence collection resources were available: Army Air Forces photo reconnaissance, division Reconnaissance Platoon, Filipino civilians from the area, several guerrilla units, and – the source of the most valuable intelligence – escaped internees. It appears there was no mechanism or time to disseminate lessons learned in regard to the Cabanatuan raid.

Aerial photos were helpful, showing up to date details of the camp's layout, barriers, Japanese positions, vegetation, approach routes, etc. They did not, however, provide sufficient details of enemy positions and obstacles, how much concealment and obstruction vegetation provided, depth of streams, trafficability of roads, or the construction details of buildings.

The Reconnaissance Platoon could provide last-minute details of enemy disposition, although it would have to move in extremely close and its discovery could warn the enemy of what was afoot.

Civilians and guerrillas were valuable as they could literally walk past the camp and collect a great deal of useful information. They were, however, of unknown quality and prone to exaggeration; they could report mistaken impressions of what they saw, sometimes reported more what they thought wanted to be heard rather than what they had actually seen, and did not always understand what was militarily important. They were however helpful for the terrain and routes in the area.

The recently escaped internees were invaluable as they were able to provide precise details of the camp's layout and buildings and the guards' quality, their posts and their routine as well as the condition of the inmates.

The guerrilla units in the Los Baños area were represented by several different groups and were under only a nebulous central command.

American troops make their way through a lightly vegetated area. The jungle around Los Baños was much denser.

The different groups were of varying quality, some being better organized and equipped than others. Their combat capabilities and motivations were very different. Some responded to US command while others were merely local warlords who sometimes made themselves more of nuisance than the Japanese, demanding from the locals food, taxes, labor, and recruits. Even those groups submitting to US command were not rigidly tied to it. They remained semi-independent and could by no means be relied on. They lacked higher-level tactical training, discipline, motivation (not to be confused with enthusiasm), and firepower. Their logistics and ability for sustained operations were limited. They often had their own political agendas.

Co-located with the 11th Abn Div CP was the headquarters of the GGC, which more or less controlled guerrilla units on southern Luzon, i.e., south of Manila. It coordinated guerrilla activities under Maj Day D. Vanderpool, a intelligence officer whose 5217th Reconnaissance Battalion[9] party had landed in October 1944 with the express mission of contacting, assessing,

US soldiers and Filipino guerrillas make their way through the jungle. Once guerrillas linked up with American forces, their armament greatly improved as they were supplied with modern arms and munitions.

---

9 This was a special reconnaissance unit under MacArthur's control. The parties were comprised of Americans and Filipinos.

Filipino guerrillas proved invaluable during the campaign to liberate the Philippines. They served in many capacities as guides, scouts, interpreters, laborers, porters, intelligence collectors, and combatants. At Los Baños several hundred guerrillas from different groups participated in the raid.

and supplying guerrilla groups which would cooperate with the US command. The party also relayed intelligence information by radio.

The most effective and cooperative guerrilla group in the area was the 45th Regiment, Hunters ROTC, under LtCol Honorio K. Guerrero.[10] Some 30,000 guerrillas, including auxiliaries, comprised the Hunters ROTC ("Terry's Hunters").[11] Many of the leadership had been members of the Philippine Military Academy and ROTC units. Col Eleuterio "Terry" Adevoso was in overall command and was also the chief of staff of GGC. Other guerrilla units in the area and participating in the operation were Marking's Fil-American Troops, Anderson's USAFFE Bonn Military Area, President Quezon's Own Guerrillas (PQOG) Red Lion Unit, Filipino-Chinese 48th Squadron, and a *Hukbalahap* unit (communist Huks who, in most areas, refused to cooperate with Americans).

GGC had arranged for additional weapons, munitions, medical supplies, and other materials to be supplied to the guerrillas, albeit in limited amounts as they were delivered by submarine and had to be carried overland and distributed. These supplies served as a control measure. Cooperating with US forces meant that units were rewarded.

---

10 It should be noted that guerrilla unit designations such as squadron, regiment, or division offer no indication of a unit's actual size, internal organization, or capabilities. They are often much smaller and less capable and the terms were intended to mislead the enemy.

11 Hunters ROTC consisted of the 44th–49th regiments operating mainly in Batangas Province and Manila. They each consisted of a few hundred fighters and hundreds of supporting auxiliaries.

Lt Col Gustavo C. "Tabo" Ingles, the Hunters ROTC inspector general, was placed in charge of mission planning. The highly respected and hardworking officer was often employed as a troubleshooter for dealing with difficult guerrilla leaders. He began collecting intelligence by any available means. On February 10 Vanderpool called a meeting with the guerrilla staff to consider the possibility of the guerrillas freeing the internees themselves. The 11th Abn Div was preoccupied with fighting its way through the Genko Line and it was not known when it would be available. The guerrillas understood that the internees were in deteriorating condition and there were rumors of an execution order. It was decided that the guerrillas *might* be able to take the camp successfully. The main problem was what to do with the internees afterwards. They could not defend the camp from the inevitable counterattacks. The internees were in such poor condition they could not be moved on foot any distance, the guerrillas had no mass transportation means, and American lines were many miles away. With over 2,100 inmates the guerrillas knew that a mass execution could not take place quickly. If it began, they would attack the camp unilaterally as a desperation measure, perhaps saving some internees. Vanderpool ordered reconnaissance of the area and intelligence collection increased.

At great risk Col Ingles crossed Laguna de Bay by *banca* and then progressed on foot to Santa Cruz, which was secured by the Hunters ROTC. He held a meeting in the town hall on February 12 with local guerrilla commanders. Only the Marking's Fil-American commander failed to attend. Ingles presented the need to liberate the internees. Previously similar proposals had been made, but the distrust between the groups had prevented unified action. Ingles, however, possessed the tool for unification: he could provide American arms.

The groups were in general agreement on the necessity and concept of the plan, but then Col Romeo "Price" Espino raised concerns as to what would happen to the Los Baños area citizens when the Japanese retaliated. It was their practice to murder civilians in the area where a guerrilla operation was executed, on the rationale that guerrillas were among them or that they had helped the guerrillas. The meeting turned ugly, almost ending in gunplay. Ingles assured Espino and other leaders that he would recommend that post-raid attacks be launched against Japanese positions in the area to keep them off balance. This was a tentative and uncertain solution, but the guerrillas believed in the necessity of the mission and would trust in the Americans and themselves to prevent such an occurrence.

On the 13th Ingles viewed the camp itself and met with George Gray, the camp's Committee secretary, who had recently escaped. The all-night discussion fully appraised Ingles of the situation inside the camp, the guards' routine, posts, and many other aspects. The next night another meeting was held by the guerrilla leadership in Dayap. Here it was agreed that Col Guerrero of the Hunters ROTC 45th Regiment would be in overall command of the operation.

Ingles then received a radio message from GGC to send a patrol to Los Baños town to reconnoiter the beach to ensure that Duck amphibious trucks could drive across the beach and check the road access to the camp. This was to be accomplished by the night of the 16th.

It is not known whose idea it was to use amphibious vehicles, but it originated at 11th Abn Div Headquarters. Prior to their incorporation into the plan their use had to be requested from XIV Corps. Their involvement was a brilliant idea. The amphibious vehicles could swim across the lake, essentially to outflank the Japanese, drive 2 miles to the camp, evacuate the internees, and either drive back to the lake or link up with an attacking overland ground force from the west. Japanese lake shore defenses were very limited, as were patrol boats.

As a result of the guerrilla leader meetings, Ingles reported that while local guerrillas possessed the strength and ammunition to seize the camp, they could not withstand a strong Japanese counterattack, which was expected to originate from Lalakay only 1½ miles away. Vanderpool had already discussed raid options with LtGen Eichelberger commanding Eighth Army, which the 11th and GGC were now under. Eichelberger had asked him on February 8 if the guerrillas could accomplish the mission alone or if they could do it with amphibious vehicles. Vanderpool responded that he thought it would require an American combat force and amphibians to secure the camp and evacuate the internees. The American force should be

Guerrillas were haphazardly armed and equipped and their "uniforms" were even less conventional. Joining up with American troops, they would scrounge whatever bits of equipment and kit they could.

in overall control and the guerrillas would support with reconnaissance, guides, and diversionary attacks, and would help in resisting Japanese counterattacks. He also stated that the assemblage of a significantly large guerrilla force and its movement could be detected by the Japanese as they had elements scattered throughout the area making the essential surprise difficult. There were also many *Makapili* in the area. There were concerns about the internees' deteriorating condition and the confidence in the ability of the guerrillas to protect them in an overland movement. Vanderpool felt that a massacre could occur when the Japanese 8th Division swept in and aimed to inflict revenge on local civilians. At this point he also recommended that Hunters ROTC be the primary guerrilla command as it had a good staff and adequate communications. Despite his concerns, his staff went ahead planning the unilateral guerrilla rescue in the event that the Japanese commenced a mass execution. Two plans were under development from February 10, the airborne's and the GGC's. The GGC's worst-case scenario plan saw a main attack force sent to liberate the camp and then reinforcements flowing in to help resist a Japanese counterattack. There was no viable way to evacuate the weakened internees other than through American amphibian support. It was open to question if over 2,100 ill and starved internees could make it 2 miles to the lake under Japanese attack. On February 9 the division was placed under the command of Sixth Army and LtGen Kruger, who had been responsible for seizing Manila, and it was subsequently attached to XIV Corps.

Ingles' report to Vanderpool caused him to scrap the unilateral guerrilla operation and the airborne and GGC staffs began combined planning on the 14th. The GGC plan still called for the main attack to be conducted by guerrillas with a US reinforced infantry battalion coming into support. The tentative plan called for the raid to occur on February 18 at 1700hrs, rather than in the morning as actually occurred. This meant that the amphibians would have to make the initial crossing in daylight and would most likely be detected by Japanese lookouts on Mayondon Point just to the east of Los Baños town. It allowed sufficient daylight to move the freed internees to the lake and then recross in the dark. Vanderpool himself was to have arrived by *banca* at Pili the night before to take direct command of the guerrillas.

On the night of the 16th Ingles held another meeting at Pili. He informed the guerrilla leaders that there would be participation by a US paratrooper battalion and he assigned missions to each unit. The guerrillas were provided with only limited US operational details:

- A company of paratroopers would jump on a DZ southwest of the camp at 1700hrs.
- 300 US troops would arrive at 2100hrs by amphibian truck at Los Baños town and proceed to the camp.
- An artillery battalion would provide fire support from west of Calamba.

The guerrillas' roles were also spelled out. All available *bancas* would be assembled at Alabang, even if it meant seizing them, to ship munitions to the guerrillas around Los Baños. Guerrillas would be issued additional ammunition and grenades controlled by Col Ingles. They were to:

- seize and hold the camp.
- secure the DZ.
- accompany the paratroopers to the camp.
- mark the landing beach and guide the amphibians to the camp.

In addition 300 guerrillas would attack and destroy the enemy force at Calamba.

The actual operation would be conducted somewhat differently and the timing changed. Other than fire support from a single US artillery battalion, there was no mention of a reinforced infantry battalion conducting a supporting attack from the west toward Calamba. Specific missions were assigned to the various guerrilla forces. Hunters ROTC 45th Regiment would control the operation and be the main attack force for the camp. The Chinese squadron would reinforce them. The Huks would serve as their reserve and reinforce them once the camp was seized. The PQOG unit would mark the DZ and guide the paratroopers to the camp. Marking's Fil-Americans would block the route from Lalakay to halt the Japanese company stationed there. They had finally decided to participate, being drawn by the promise of munitions and not wanting to miss out on any future benefits granted by the Americans. There is virtually no information available on the strength and organization of the different guerrilla units throughout the operation. Guerrilla leaders tend to keep this to themselves fearing that they might be deployed in a detrimental manner. Guerrillas are deeply concerned about misutilization and taskings they are unable to handle. Conventional regular force commanders often downplay the importance of guerrillas, considering them irrelevant, and might waste them for no good purpose. Guerrilla commanders understand that their troops are relatives, friends, and neighbors and that the commanders will be held accountable for them.

Even though US participation was being planned by the 11th Abn Div and coordinated with the GGC, it appears that the guerrillas were moving ahead irrespective of whether or not there would be American participation. It is not known to what extent the guerrillas began deploying. Some claim they were fully deployed around the camp on the night of the 18/19th and prepared to execute the afternoon attack on the 19th. At this point the GGC advanced headquarters dispatched messengers to Col Guerrero of the 45th Regiment canceling the operation, as the tasked parachute unit and aircraft were diverted to jump on Corregidor. The reason given had no basis in fact. The 503rd PIR, which was not a part of the 11th Abn Div, had jumped onto Corregidor the morning of the 16th. It had never been tasked for the Los Baños mission and had been alerted for Corregidor on February 6. Since the Corregidor assault was known, it was probably assumed this was the reason for the delay. In fact, the attack was postponed simply because the 11th was unable to pull the units tasked for Los Baños out of the line until the 20th, the day after the guerrillas planned to attack the camp.

This false start was good for the guerrillas, although no doubt frustrating. They were able to collect more intelligence, became more familiar with the terrain, and probably refined their deployment. There was, though, a danger that the Japanese could have discovered the deployment even if they did not understand its full extent and intent. *Makapili* informers too could have reported the movements. This would have alerted not only the camp guards but other units in the area, and perhaps even caused reinforcement and occupation of additional positions. Japanese forces, however, were concentrated in several areas, although they did have some units in outlying locations. They had little control over the countryside and scattered villages and towns.

FEBRUARY 21 1945

Final plan outlined

The final plan

The 11th Abn Div staff, working closely with the GGC, was hurriedly finalizing the new plan. In the meantime, a radioman from the 511th Airborne Signal Company, Tech 3 (S Sgt) John Fulton, was smuggled via *banca* across the lake to Tranca where he set up his SCR-536 radio with the PQOG's Red Lion Unit on the 11th. Ingles and Fulton relayed messages via runners as Fulton maintained contact with the division staff. However, as this required messengers to make six-hour round trips, Ingles ordered Fulton to relocate to Nanhaya on the night of the 18th. Vanderpool would soon arrive and the operation's execution date was approaching.

On February 21, Ingles received word from Espino, "Have received reliable information that that Japs have Los Baños scheduled for massacre." It was immediately transmitted to the division staff. Preparations were stepped up. The attack would be conducted in the morning rather than the afternoon, to catch the guards undertaking calisthenics. The amtracs would not simply deliver the rest of the parachute battalion, but would evacuate the internees over-water instead of leaving the diversionary force to extract them, although overland was still an option.

The 11th Abn Div plan for the Los Baños rescue was divided into five phases:

Phase I – Reconnaissance of Los Baños camp and mission planning.

Phase II – Infiltration by Reconnaissance Platoon and guerrillas, securing of the beach landing site and DZ, and positioning to neutralize sentries.

Phase III – Delivery of the parachute company, movement to and attack on the camp, and organization of internees for evacuation.

Phase IV – Arrival of amphibious force and evacuation of internees and troops to US lines.

Phase V – Diversionary ground attack from west to draw enemy forces and meet a counterattack.

The basic plan evolved to accomplish the mission. The Reconnaissance Platoon would cross Laguna de Bay aboard *bancas* and link up with guerrillas on the night of February 21. The scouts, assisted by guerrillas, would split into several groups. They would mark the amtrac beach landing site and reconnoiter the route to the camp, mark the DZ and establish a drop site where messages could be dropped from L-4 liaison aircraft. Five teams would initiate the attack on the perimeter guard posts and the

Two 75mm M1A1 pack howitzers of Battery D, 457th Glider Field Artillery Battalion were landed by LVT(4) amphibious tractors on San Antonio beach. This was the only fire support available to 1st Battalion, 511th Parachute Infantry Regiment attacking Los Baños camp.

exercising guards when the paratroopers tumbled out of their aircraft at 0700hrs – H-Hour – on February 23.

A reinforced rifle company would parachute onto the DZ on the camp's northeast side. It would not assemble as a company; instead each platoon would gather and then press on with its mission irrespective of the rest of the company. They would move to the camp as quickly as possible and reinforce the scouts and guerrillas if they had not yet neutralized all guards. Then they would organize the internees for evacuation and establish a defensive perimeter.

The rest of the parachute battalion, reinforced by engineers and two howitzers, would land by amtrac at San Antonio 1 mile east of Mayondon Point rather than the west as originally planned, as it was learned on the 21st that the Japanese had reoccupied the hilly point and a position near the original landing site. They would remain mounted so long as there was no resistance. If they met resistance they would dismount and engage, supported by the amtracs' considerable machine-gun firepower. Reaching the camp, one company would deploy to the south as a blocking force and the other to the west to block any enemy from that direction. An engineer platoon would establish roadblocks. The howitzers would remain on the beach with a rifle platoon to provide fire support. The original plan called for the internees to be marched west on Highway 1 to meet the diversionary force and be picked up by trucks. The airborne battalion would bring up the rear and the amtracs would return across the lake empty. It was feared that fire from the lower west shore and patrol boats would endanger the internees if they were carried by amtracs. There was a three-hour limit for remaining at the camp and by then they had to move out, as the Japanese could attack by that time.

The overland diversionary attack by a reinforced glider battalion would move down National Highway 1 to the San Juan River the night before and at H-Hour would attack toward the Lechería Hills and support guerrillas securing Calamba, as well as blocking enemy forces approaching from the south. It would bring enough trucks to evacuate the internees. However, engineers reported that the roads east of San Juan were in too poor a condition, with too many bridges destroyed, to use trucks, so it was now tentatively decided to evacuate the internees by amtrac (though this change appears not to have been clearly understood by all involved). There was still an option to link up with the diversionary force if the lake evacuation proved impractical. This task force included two artillery battalions, a tank destroyer company, and engineers.

Air cover in the form of 27 orbiting P-38 Lightning fighters of the 347th Fighter Group[12] based at McGuire Field, San José, on Mindoro would attack enemy forces moving toward the camp. They were tasked with keeping the Japanese down and off roads. Forcing the Japanese to cross-country movement would delay them further. Fighters had strafed some Japanese positions near the camp the day before the raid. Guerrilla units would deploy south and west to block enemy movements and cover the withdrawal.

The planning and execution of the operation was directly under 11th Abn Div. Both Sixth Army and XIV Corps were "out of the loop." Although Gen Swing oversaw the operation, the commander of the 511th PIR, LtCol Robert Soule, was the immediate "commander on the ground." He also directly commanded Soule Task Force (TF), the diversionary force. Los Baños Task Force, the airborne and amphibious force, was under the command of Maj Henry Burgess of the 1/511th PIR. He answered to Soule, but they would never establish radio contact. LtCol Joseph Gibbs commanding the 672nd Amphibious Tractor Battalion was subordinate to Maj Burgess, an oddity of command. A mutual understanding was developed between them. Gibbs was responsible for his amphibians, but Burgess was the maneuver commander.

Sunrise would be a few minutes before 0615hrs. Sunset was at 1802hrs. This provided about 13 hours of darkness for the *bancas* to travel on the lake as part of the mission's preparation. The nights would be moonless. The weather was clear, with high temperatures in the upper 80-degree Fahrenheit range by day and at night in the low 70s. Winds were light and from the south.

---

12 Fighters of this group downed Admiral Isoroku Yamanoto's transport in 1943.

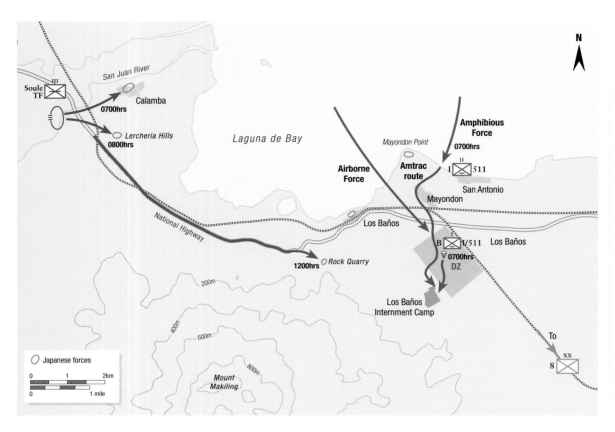

Operational area of the
Los Baños raid

The objective

Los Baños internment camp was built on the athletic fields of the former Agricultural College of the Philippines 2 miles south of Los Baños town and Laguna de Bay. Passing east-to-west through the town were National Highway 1 and a railroad, a branch of which turned southeast and ran less than ¾ mile east of the camp. Most of the terrain immediately around the camp was fairly level and open, consisting of either uncultivated fields or rice paddies. There were scattered bands and groves of trees and brush. Streams and gullies ran northeastward from the camp and this included a ravine up to 40ft deep running from the area of the main gate. The main gate asphalt road, Pili Lane, ran to the railroad station. Boot Creek ran around the camp's south and west sides and its deep banks were thickly vegetated. The west and southwest sides of the camp were located in the most rugged terrain. These areas were overgrown with trees and brush reaching to the base of the forested 3,576ft-high Mount Makiling (spelled Maquiling in period documents) to the southwest, an inactive volcano. The camp's elevation was 130–150ft above sea level.

The camp covered about 60 acres and was of irregular shape, being approximately 600 x 800 yards. It was surrounded by double barbed wire fences, the inner being 4ft high and the outer 6ft. Some fence sections were clad in *sawali* (a form of mat-like wall made from woven split bamboo) to deny observation. This hampered some of the attackers as they could not see if any guards were beyond the fence. It was easy to break through and did not reinforce the fences. The main gate was centered on the northeast side and there was another on the southwest. There were other secondary gates on the southeast and there were nine guard posts that consisted of earth and log pillboxes manned by one to five men, as well as a tenth post outside the camp to the southeast. There were also roving guards. The commandant's headquarters and guard barracks connected by the arms room were just inside the main gate.

The camp was divided into two sections, "Hell's Half-Acre" or "Hell's Hole," where most of the inmates lived, in the north portion, and "Vatican City" or the "Holy City" in the southwest containing the missionaries, priests, nuns, and other religious. A *sawali* fence ("Walls of Jericho") separated the two areas; the inmates had been kept segregated until about six months previously.

The 26 barracks were on ground-level concrete slabs and measured 30 x 198ft. The wood-frame barracks had high thatched nipa palm roofs, some reinforced by a bamboo framework overlaying the nipa to secure it in high winds. The side walls were made of *sawali* fitted with large windows with *sawali* drop shutters, which served as awnings for rain protection. There was a long central corridor with eight rooms on each side and a door at each end. The rooms were for families or small groups of single men or women. Every two barracks had each six showers, sinks with faucets, and men's and women's toilets. The buildings were highly flammable and there were no electric lights. Blackout was mandatory.

Existing college buildings included 15 concrete buildings, five two-story dormitories, and 30 faculty cottages. Baker Memorial Hall, a monolithic two-story concrete gymnasium, was just outside the camp's north corner. This is where the original group of inmates was quartered when it first arrived. It was occasionally used as rest quarters for transiting Japanese units, but was unoccupied at the time of the attack.

The enemy

Even the escaped inmates had only a rough idea of the strength of the guard. It was estimated at 150–250. Their combat qualities were unknown. The escapees could not report on their experience level as they simply stood guard. The planners considered them to be trained combat troops, but many were older soldiers and those recovering from wounds or illness. The resistance they would present might be for self-defense more than to hold the camp. If the initial surprise attack on the guards and the calisthenics formation felled enough of them, resistance might be disorganized.

Of more concern were the forces outside the camp. Some 3,000 yards west of the camp was a rock quarry on the Dampalit River. A company of up to 200 men with two 10.5cm howitzers and four machine-guns was stationed there. There was a 20-man outpost on the Los Baños wharf and nearby were two 7cm guns covering the lake. These were west of Mayondon Point jutting out into the lake. The amtracs would land at San Antonio east of the point and 2½ miles from the camp. Well west of the objective was an

80-man roadblock with two 7.5cm guns in the twin Lechería Hills on National Highway 1 to the south of Calamba and east of the San Juan River. The diversionary force would attack this position. Major concern was caused by the 8,000–10,000 combat-experienced and rested troops of MajGen Shizuo Yokoyama's 8th Division (17th and 31st Infantry, 8th Field Artillery Regiments)[13] bivouacked in the hills south of Santo Tomás–Alaminos–San Pablo. It had served in Manchuria from 1939–44 and arrived on Luzon in September 1944. Its 5th Infantry had been destroyed on Leyte. One of its battalions could reach the camp in 1½ hours if dispatched immediately. Realistically it would take more time for the Japanese to assess the situation and make a decision. Nonetheless the division posed a threat if the evacuation became bogged down for some reason.

Some danger was seen in the Japanese patrol boats on Laguna de Bay. They knew the guerrillas used the lake as a means of travel. There were small patrol boat bases at Talim, at Punta at the tip of the large peninsula thrusting south into the lake, and at Calamba Island in the lake's southwest portion. Although a threat to *bancas*, they posed no noteworthy danger to the amtracs even if all boats, of which there were few, were massed.

---

13 The 8th Division is often incorrectly nicknamed the "Tiger Division." "Tiger" was the codename for the 19th Division which fought in central Luzon. The 8th Division was codenamed "Cedar" (*Sugi*).

THE RAID

Initial deployments

Besides the various guerrilla elements, there were seven US forces which had to position themselves to execute their missions at precisely 0700hrs, February 23. On the 20th units began to deploy.

On February 18 Maj Henry A. "Hank" Burgess commanding 1st Battalion, 511th PIR had been contacted by Lt Col Edward H. Lahti, the regimental commander. Fighting toward Ft McKinley, he was told to pull back to a "rest area" and report to the division CP in Parañaque. Lahti had only taken command of the 511th on the 8th when its commander was killed. Burgess had taken over 1st Battalion in early January when its commander had been relieved on Leyte. The 26-year-old officer had been the division assistant G-3 and was highly thought of. He would be the ideal leader for the mission, which required thorough planning and decisiveness. At the CP he was informed of the mission, learning that he had only five days to prepare. The G-2 and G-3 sections committed all their resources. Planning would be carried out under complete secrecy. There were no written operation orders; the orders were prepared *after* the event for historical files. Peter Mills arrived from Los Banos on the 19th and contributed his information. Only the unit commanders involved and certain key individuals were aware of the mission. Others would not learn of it until the 21st. Swing, the division staff, and the battalion commanders understood that there were risks, but felt the odds were in their favor.

1/511th PIR, minus Company B, marched from its rest area south on Highway 1 along the shore of Laguna de Bay, reaching a position outside Mamatid on the 21st. It bivouacked in the jungle, remaining hidden. A platoon of 20 engineers and two 75mm howitzers with 20 artillerymen joined it there.

Four days prior to D-Day, it needed to be determined which company would jump in. Company B, 1/511th was selected purely because it had the highest strength, 93 out of an authorized 127. After being pulled out of the line, the soldiers were trucked to New Bilibid prison on Laguna de Bay. Here

LOS BAÑOS RAID TASK FORCES, FEBRUARY 23, 1945

Los Baños Task Force
Parachute-delivered
Company B, 1st Battalion, 511th PIR
Light Machine-Gun Platoon, HQ Company, 1st Battalion, 511th PIR
squad, Company C (Parachute), 127th Airborne Engineer Battalion
flight, 65th Troop Carrier Squadron (65th TCS)

Overwater-delivered by LVT
1st Battalion (–), 511th PIR
detachment (two howitzers), Battery D, 457th PFAB
platoon (–), Company C (Parachute), 127th Airborne Engineer Battalion
Provisional Reconnaissance Platoon, 11th Abn Div
672nd Amphibian Tractor Battalion (–)

Guerrilla detachments linking up in vicinity of Los Baños
45th Regiment, Hunters ROTC
Marking's Fil-Americans
President Quezon's Own Guerrillas (PQOG)
48th Chinese Squadron
Villegas Group, *Hukbalahaps*

Soule Task Force
188th GIR (minus 2nd Battalion)
2nd Battalion, 511th PIR (TF Reserve – not committed)
472nd Field Artillery Battalion (105mm Howitzer, Tractor-Drawn)
675th Glider Field Artillery Battalion (105mm Howitzer)
Company B, 637th Tank Destroyer Battalion
Company C (Parachute) (–), 127th Airborne Engineer Battalion
detachment, 1011th Engineer Treadway Bridge Company
47th Regiment, Hunters ROTC

they rested and on the 21st were briefed. Most were proud they had been selected and understood the importance of the rescue, but some had doubts and the words "suicide mission" were muttered.

Three young guerrillas had attached themselves to the company during the Manila fighting and had become accepted by the paratroopers, one per platoon. One of the NCOs approached the commanding officer, 1st Lt John M. Ringler, and asked if the Filipinos could jump with them. Surprisingly he agreed, possibly understanding that his company could use reinforcement. They were given three hours of parachute orientation and declared ready to go. The battalion light machine-gun platoon under 2nd Lt Walter Hettinger was attached on the 22nd, with one section attached to two of the rifle platoons. The platoon would revert to battalion-control when the amtracs arrived.

The 317th Troop Carrier Group, which had supported all other parachute drops in the Pacific, was committed to resupplying the 503rd PIR fighting on Corregidor. On the 20th it was learned that the 65th Troop

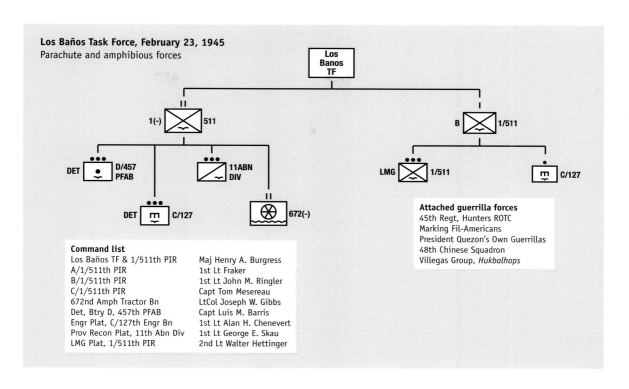

Los Baños Task Force, February 23, 1945
Parachute and amphibious forces

Attached guerrilla forces
45th Regt, Hunters ROTC
Marking Fil-Americans
President Quezon's Own Guerrillas
48th Chinese Squadron
Villegas Group, *Hukbalhaps*

Command list

Los Baños TF & 1/511th PIR	Maj Henry A. Burgress
A/1/511th PIR	1st Lt Fraker
B/1/511th PIR	1st Lt John M. Ringler
C/1/511th PIR	Capt Tom Mesereau
672nd Amph Tractor Bn	LtCol Joseph W. Gibbs
Det, Btry D, 457th PFAB	Capt Luis M. Barris
Engr Plat, C/127th Engr Bn	1st Lt Alan H. Chenevert
Prov Recon Plat, 11th Abn Div	1st Lt George E. Skau
LMG Plat, 1/511th PIR	2nd Lt Walter Hettinger

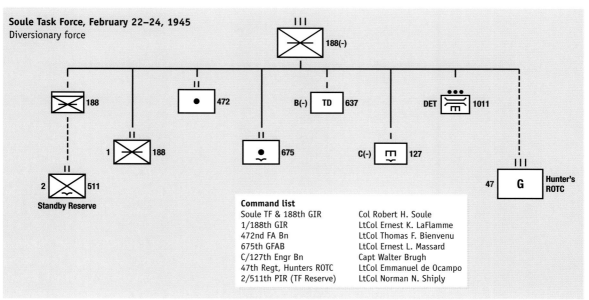

Soule Task Force, February 22–24, 1945
Diversionary force

Standby Reserve

Command list

Soule TF & 188th GIR	Col Robert H. Soule
1/188th GIR	LtCol Ernest K. LaFlamme
472nd FA Bn	LtCol Thomas F. Bienvenu
675th GFAB	LtCol Ernest L. Massard
C/127th Engr Bn	Capt Walter Brugh
47th Regt, Hunters ROTC	LtCol Emmanuel de Ocampo
2/511th PIR (TF Reserve)	LtCol Norman N. Shiply

Carrier Squadron (65th TCS) of the 433rd Troop Carrier Group at Hill Field, San José on Mindoro would support the drop. On the 21st the squadron commander, Capt Donald G. Anderson, and his operations officer arrived in a C-47 at Nichols Field. The field was bomb-damaged and the 11th Abn Div's engineers rushed to repair it. After being briefed by the division staff, Anderson over-flew the camp at 5,000ft and identified

65TH TROOP CARRIER SQUADRON

The 65th TCS was activated at Bowman Field, Kentucky on December 12, 1942 and equipped with 18 C-47A transports. After training in various locations it deployed to New Guinea in July 1943, and operated from several different fields on New Guinea and Biak. From January 24 to February 27, 1945, the time of the raid, it was based at Hill Field on Mindoro. It was one of the six squadrons (65th–70th TCS) of Col John H. Lackey Jr's 433rd Troop Carrier Group, and was commanded during the Los Baños raid by Capt Donald G. Anderson. All of the parachute drops in the Pacific were conducted by the 317th Troop Carrier Group, with the exception of Los Baños. This operation was flown by half of the 65th TCS, with Lackey accompanying the flight, though the unit had last dropped paratroopers when in training for the jump school at Ft Benning, Georgia. For its timely and precision delivery at Los Baños, the unit was awarded the Distinguished Unit Citation inscribed "Laguna de Bay, Luzon, 23 February 1945." The squadron remained on Luzon until returning to the United States and was deactivated in January 1946. It was reactivated as a Reserve unit in 1947, called to active duty in 1951, and returned to the Reserves in 1953. It again served on active duty briefly in 1962 and was deactivated in 1966. Redesignated the 65th Airlift Squadron, the unit was reactivated in 1992 and remains active in Hawaii providing VIP airlift throughout the Pacific with C-37 (Gulfstream V) and C-40 Clipper (Boeing 737) executive transports.

the DZ. On the 22nd eight more C-47s arrived at Nichols. The aircraft were refueled and the crew chiefs checked them over.

Late in the afternoon of the 22nd, after a hot meal, Company B was trucked to Nichols Field. Parachutes were issued, equipment rigged, door bundles packed, and 15-man sticks were assigned to each transport. Some men carried extra submachine guns and grenades for guerrillas. The machine-gunners removed the tracers to prevent fires among the inflammable barracks. The paratroopers were thoroughly briefed and every man given a detailed map of the camp. Normal jump altitude was 1,000–1,200ft, but on this occasion they would jump from 400–500ft so that they could reach the ground as fast as possible and land close together. At such a low altitude reserve parachutes could not be deployed, but they were worn anyway to instill confidence. From 500ft the descent would require approximately 25 seconds. The aircraft would fly in three "V"s of three aircraft, with each following "V" slightly higher than the first. The paratroopers and crews spent a restless night bedded down under the aircraft wings.

Several engineer elements participated.[14] On February 20 an engineer patrol reconnoitered the highway from Muntinlupa to the San Juan River and discovered that several bridges needed to be repaired or replaced. Repair work on the northern bridges began. That same night four engineers traveled by *banca* from Binan to Pili, 15 miles east of Los Baños. They reconnoitered the shore back to San Antonio, selected an amtrac landing beach there, and radioed the information to division.

A platoon of Company C (Parachute), 127th Airborne Engineer Battalion was attached to 1/511th PIR. Its mission was to establish roadblocks. One

---

14 Unfortunately documents do not provide the designations of engineer subunits.

of its squads was attached to Company B, 1/511th PIR at the last minute as additional reinforcement. Originally the entire platoon was to jump in, but the number of troops and amount of demolitions prevented this. The rest of the platoon was to support a rifle company establishing two roadblocks, so it would in fact be more effective for it to accompany the company aboard the amtracs. The platoon leader accompanied the squad to Nichols Field, to await the arrival of C3 plastic explosives, which never arrived. With no time remaining to rejoin his platoon at Mamatid, he joined the squad for the jump. The rest of Company C accompanied the Soule TF.

The Reconnaissance Platoon set out on its dangerous infiltration on the night of the 21st. After a detailed briefing in which the platoon was broken down into groups for D-Day specific missions, they boarded three *bancas* at Mamatid for a two-to-three hour trip across the lake. 1st Lt George Skau departed with three scouts and three war correspondents at 2000hrs. Fifteen minutes later Sgt Squires left with five men. The rest of the platoon, 23 men with most of their crew-served weapons and equipment, departed in a large sailing *banca* after a two-hour delay caused by a broken rudder. Light winds resulted in an eight-hour crossing for Skau and one of ten hours for Squires. They made it just before sunrise. They moved to Nanhaya and met the guerrillas at the schoolhouse. Skau learned the latest information from them as well as from internees Edwards and Zeroulakos. With the various guerrilla leaders they further developed their attack plan. The bulk of the platoon in the last *banca* had not arrived.

This small unit had the most elaborate and complex plan of the various elements. The platoon would deploy in six teams, if the rest of the platoon arrived, with 190 guerrillas detailed. Six to eight guerrillas were attached to most teams. Sgt Turner's team with PQOC and Huks would mark the DZ with green smoke at 0658hrs. Sgt Hahn's team had a company of Marking's Fil-American guerrillas and would mark the San Antonio amtrac landing beach with green smoke as well as securing the beachhead. Sgts Angus, Call, and Town, and Lt Skau led teams tailored to take out guard posts on the north and west sides. One team would cut through the fence and rush the arms room. Lt Skau's team would attack the main gate guard post. Sgt Squires' team, with six scouts, internee Edwards, and 20 guerrillas, was assigned the posts on the camp's northwest perimeter. All of the guerrillas in the assault teams were Hunters ROTC. A scratch team was assembled with radio operator Fulton, Zervoulakos, and seven guerrillas and detailed to block guards fleeing south. Skau made use of every available man, even escaped internees.

In the early evening hours of the 22nd the large *banca*, with the rest of the platoon, arrived at Nanhaya after a harrowing day becalmed and fearing discovery by patrol boats. The still irate scouts were briefed and the teams started deploying after dark. Skau cautioned all involved to use extreme stealth, not to return fire if guards or patrols fired at their noise, and to take any casualties with them. He was concerned that if they were discovered the Japanese might initiate a massacre. All of the teams would encounter difficulties reaching their positions and would require hours to do so.

The diversionary force, named the Soule Task Force after the commander of the 188th GIR, LtCol Robert H. "Shorty" Soule, had been pulled out of the line and assembled near Parañaque. It left its 2nd Battalion engaged. The 1st Battalion (under LtCol Ernest LaFlamme) would be the only infantry force committed to the diversion. The task force also consisted of the 675th Glider Field Artillery Battalion (GFAB) and attached 472nd Field Artillery Battalion. Both battalions were armed with 105mm howitzers, but the glider battalion had only the "snub-nosed" M3. This weapon had only a 8,295-yard range, which was about 1,500 yards shorter than the 75mm pack howitzer that equipped the division's other battalions, and was capable of reaching only two-thirds the range of the standard 105mm M2A1. The 472nd was armed with M2A1s. A tank destroyer company with 76mm gun-armed M18 Hellcat tank destroyers was also attached along with bridging engineers and divisional trucks. Just before nightfall on the 22nd, Soule TF quietly occupied positions along the San Juan River and prepared to advance as noisily as possible. The artillery battalions set up to fire on the Lechería Hills and the rock quarry. The M2A1 howitzers could not quite reach Los Baños. The 2/511th PIR (under LtCol Frank S. Holcombe) was tasked as the TF Reserve and bivouacked outside Parañaque. Elements of the task force were delayed by destroyed bridges until engineers constructed by-passes. The 675th GFAB set up north of Calamba and the 472nd west of the highway.

The Old Bilibid prison was not far from Santo Tomás University inside Manila. Both contained thousands of civilian internees when liberated on February 3, 1945. It would be in the New Bilibid prison, some miles away, that the liberated Los Baños internees would be housed after their rescue three weeks later.

The task force linked up with LtCol Emmanuel de Ocampo's 47th Regiment of Hunters ROTC. They were provided with four 2½-ton trucks and the entire unit was jammed aboard and trucked to Calamba to protect the task force's flank. Calamba, a mile northeast of the Lechería Hills, was infested with *Makapili*.

The 672nd Amphibian Tractor Battalion assembled south of Manila and drove along the lake beach to Mamatid. Roaring ashore before dark on the 22nd, watched by doubtful paratroopers, it sparked fears that the exceedingly noisy amtracs would alert informers or be heard by the Japanese across the lake. It refueled and pulled maintenance.

All elements were in place on the night of February 22. The Reconnaissance Platoon and its accompanying guerrillas would move into their final positions just before H-Hour. The troops to be delivered by aircraft and amtracs would have to be up hours before H-Hour and on their way to their destination. At New Bilibid prison medical personnel, cooks, administrators, and truck drivers were preparing to receive over 2,100 sick and starving civilians.

The division staff experienced a sleepless night. At midnight they received a report from a P-61 Black Widow night fighter patrolling over Laguna de Bay. "Hundreds of truck headlights" were seen approaching Los Baños from the east and returning east. There was a fear that the operation had been compromised and the internees were being moved. An Alamo Scout team in the area reported that it had been told that 3,000 Japanese had reinforced the Los Baños area. Swing decided to ignore the reports. If the internees were being moved there was nothing that could be done to halt it. At this point the internees were best served by continuing the operation as planned. Ordering the units to launch as soon as possible would only completely disrupt the precise timing, with elements arriving at different times unsupported. The deployed units were not even told of the headlight report to prevent them from jumping the time schedule on their own. Swing did, however, alert 2/511th PIR to be ready to deploy to support Soule TF if necessary. It was later found that these reports, both much exaggerated, referred to a reinforcement of the Mount Makiling area by the Japanese 8th Division. The amtracs at Mamatid were reported to the Japanese, but they were thought to be tanks and assessed to support an attack down Highway 1. As it turned out the Japanese thought the Soule TF diversionary attack was this main attack. They did not move to counterattack it, but were dug in to meet the offensive.

Swing and his staff arrived at Mamatid to observe the departure of the amtrac force. Swing would later be overhead in an L-4 aircraft. LtCol Soule with the diversionary force was now the overall mission commander; his command included the amphibious, parachute, and reconnaissance forces, with which he had no radio contact. The liaison officer with the Soule TF callsigns and frequencies had never joined up with Burgess before departing Mamatid.

Inside Los Baños camp the inmates had no hint that their deliverance was fast approaching. It had been just another routine night for the guards.

FEBRUARY 23 1945

0515hrs Amtrac column moves out

FEBRUARY 23 1945

0600–0630hrs Company B's C-47As take off

FEBRUARY 23 1945

0658hrs The Reconnaissance Platoon pops green smoke

The attack

The first element to begin moving in the early morning hours of Friday, February 23, was the amphibious force. The troops were up at 0400hrs and loaded by 0500hrs. At 0515hrs the columns of amtracs rolled noisily over the beach into the dark lake. The 54 amtracs spread into a formation of three columns of 18 vehicles and churned their way eastward at 5mph. At 0550hrs they made a 90-degree turn south. This placed them safely distant from the west shore where there were Japanese outposts. Navigation was by dead reckoning (based on compass and time traveled at a specified speed). Amtracs did not mount compasses so handheld compasses were used. The crews were not trained for long-distance navigation at night; amtracs were intended strictly as ship-to-shore vehicles, normally traveling only a couple of thousand yards at the most after launching from landing ships, tank (LSTs) to a shore within sight. At 0620hrs they made another slight course change to aim toward the San Antonio beach. As the sun rose they could make out the beach only minutes away. Low overhead the nine C-47s roared over. The waterborne paratroopers were surprised at how low they were.

At Nichols Field Company B too had been up since 0400 hrs and had eaten K-rations beside their planes. The reinforced company was chuted up and loaded down with weapons and ammunition. The roughly 15-man sticks boarded the transports and buckled in. The engines cranked over at 0600hrs and the planes taxied to the runway. The last transport was off the ground at 0630hrs and the column of planes made an orbit of the airfield and broke into three "V"s, each of three aircraft, flying east toward the dark shape of Laguna de Bay at 0640hrs. Los Baños was 20 minutes away. The lead "V"

A Douglas C-47A transport could carry up to 19 paratroopers. For the Los Baños jump Company B, 1st Battalion, 511th Parachute Infantry Regiment loaded approximately 15 paratroopers in each of the nine transports. The jump door is off the left edge of the photograph.

was at 400ft, the second at 450ft, and the last at 500ft. Even at their low altitude there was sufficient light from the rising sun to provide clear vision. They turned south and could easily make out Mayondon Point bluntly jutting out into the lake. As the transports passed over the amtrac formation, which could be seen by the jumpmasters standing in the doors, the paratroopers were going through the sequence of jump commands. At 0655hrs the red warning lights beside the jump doors lit up. The jumpmasters shouted, "Five minutes!" Lt Ringler standing in the door of the lead aircraft spotted green smoke on the DZ beside the camp. It was 0658hrs. The green light flashed on and he shouted, "Go!" The paratroopers tumbled out at less than one-second intervals. They osculated perhaps three times before hitting the ground and could hear the crackle of gun fire from the camp. Their job done, the nine transports continued south to their home base on Mindoro in time for a late celebratory breakfast.

At 0658hrs green smoke grenades were popped on the San Antonio beach and the amtracs broke up into nine columns of six vehicles, coming ashore in six waves. The navigation had been dead on for the 1-hour 14-minute trip. Hilly Mayondon Point a mile to the east, a Japanese position, opened up with ineffective small-arms fire. Churning sand with engines snorting, the amtracs rumbled ashore dead on time. Not a single one had broken down or separated. Scouts and guerrillas directed them to the road. Two scouts boarded to guide them to the camp as the last of the parachute canopies disappeared below the trees. A platoon of Company A was offloaded for beachhead security, as were two 75mm howitzers towed by jeeps. A small guerrilla company remained with them. These guns would soon start shelling Mayondon Point, from which fire was increasing. The amtracs moved on toward the camp. The roaring engines prevented them from hearing gunfire there.

DOUGLAS C-47A SKYTRAIN TRANSPORT

The C-47A was the most widely used transport during World War II. Known as the Dakota to the British and also as the Gooney Bird (mostly in Europe), it was a beefed-up, military version of the DC-3 airliner. Although the DC-3's maiden flight was in 1935, the C-47A did not become operational until 1941. It was a true workhorse of the war, being the aerial equivalent of the 2½-ton cargo truck. It had a crew of three, the pilot and co-pilot and the crew chief, who was responsible for cargo/passenger loading and unloading. The twin 1,250hp engine transport had a 1,500-mile range and could carry 6,000lb of cargo, or 28 combat-equipped troops, or 18 litters, or 15–19 paratroopers. Paratroopers exited from the cargo door on the left side. Six large equipment/supply drop bundles could be attached to bomb shackles beneath the wings and fuselage, but this capability was not used during the Los Baños jump.

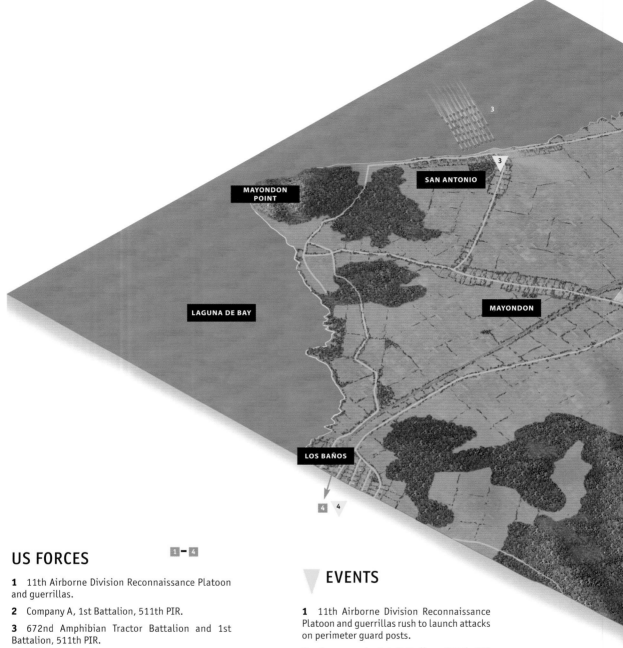

US FORCES

1 - 4

1 11th Airborne Division Reconnaissance Platoon and guerrillas.

2 Company A, 1st Battalion, 511th PIR.

3 672nd Amphibian Tractor Battalion and 1st Battalion, 511th PIR.

4 Soule TF

JAPANESE FORCES

1

1 Japanese 8th Division, deployed to the east, southeast and south of the internment camp.

EVENTS

1 11th Airborne Division Reconnaissance Platoon and guerrillas rush to launch attacks on perimeter guard posts.

2 Company A, 1st Battalion, 511th PIR begins to jump from nine 65th TCS C-47A transports.

3 672nd Amphibian Tractor Battalion arrives on San Antonio Beach with 1st Battalion, 511th PIR.

4 Soule TF commences its diversionary attack to the west across the San Juan River.

LIBERATION COMMENCES

0700 HOURS, FEBRUARY 23, 1945

H-Hour – 0700 hours – on February 23, 1945, saw the start of the operation to liberate the Los Baños internment camp. The Reconnaissance Platoon and their guerrilla allies launched an assault on the camp, taking out the perimeter guard posts and neutralizing the guards, while Company A of the 1st Battalion, 511th PIR began to jump from their transports to support the troops on the ground. At San Antonio, the am-tracs that were intended to evacuate the freed internees started to come ashore. Meanwhile, 7 miles east, the Soule TF commenced their diversion, striking out against the Japanese forces across the San Juan River.

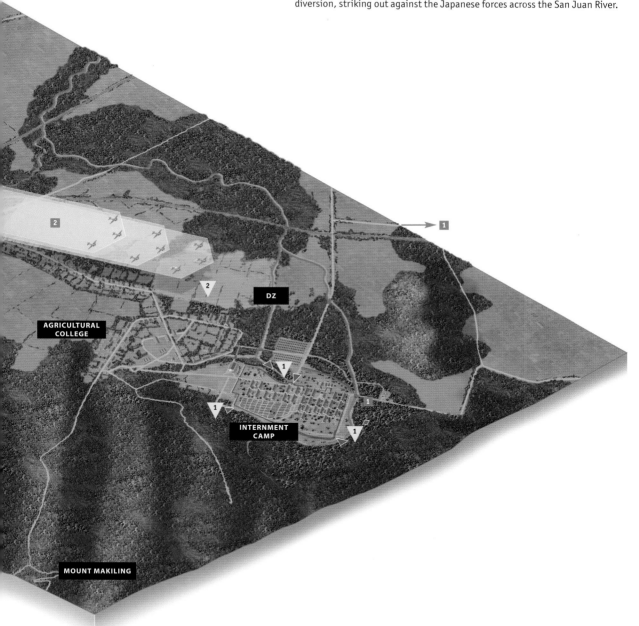

Besides US-supplied weapons and captured Japanese arms, guerrillas made extensive use of bolo machetes, both as a tool and as a weapon. This particular model is of traditional design. More modern ones were made from automobile leaf springs.

Paratroopers exit the left troop door of a C-47A, typically at a rate of one every second. The T-5 parachute was 28ft in diameter.

For the reconnaissance teams approaching the camp, events did not go as smoothly as they did for the paratroopers and amphibians. A potentially disastrous incident occurred as the scout/guerrilla teams moved into position in the darkness. Sgt Squires' team with six scouts, Edwards, and the remaining half-dozen guerrillas skirted around the camp's west side near the old faculty cottages, apparently now occupied by Filipino civilians. The team had started with 20 guerrillas but many had been separated, either intentionally or by accident. It was 15 minutes before H-Hour. A dog unexpectedly attacked one of the guerrillas, who drew his pistol and fired, felling the animal. It must have sounded like a cannon shot in the pre-dawn darkness. After freezing and holding their breaths, they moved on. There was no response, not even questioning shouts from guards. The off-duty guards would be falling in for morning exercise and the inmates were readying for roll call. The team reached its position with only minutes to spare.

Sgt Town's team too was approaching the camp's southwest corner when four guards were spotted crossing a field just as the attack opened. All four were gunned down with a BAR and a fifth was shot as he was crawling through the wire to escape.

Three other teams were not yet in position. It took hours for the teams to reach their positions owing to flooded rice paddies, gullies, dense vegetation, and the pitch-dark night. The guerrilla guides were not always familiar with the way.

Lt Skau's team, heading for the main gate and with the platoon's only machine-gun, was at least 200 yards from its target when the shooting started. They continued on, made their way through the gate, and seized the arms room gunning down guards. Sgt Call's team had only entered the wide ravine near the camp hospital when the attack was launched. As they scrambled toward the camp, they were taken under machine-gun fire from north of the main gate. Call took a bullet in the shoulder and a man's nose was nicked by a grenade fragment. The attack found Sgt Angus and his team charging totally exposed toward the rear gate over a clear field. The guard post was deserted, but they shot two guards inside the wire.

Call's, Squires', Town's, and Angus' teams were soon fully engaged, firing into the camp and guard posts and shooting down fleeing Japanese. Some guards were holding out in the main gate pillbox and Call requested Company B to drop 60mm mortar rounds on it. His team then closed in, grenading the position. This went on for 15 minutes before they started cutting through the fences. Many of the guerrillas did not enter the camp, but chased after running guards, shooting them down or hacking them to death with bolo machetes.

Squires' team used grenades to force their way into the camp through the northwest corner. Here Edwards, the former internee, was nicked in the shins by bullet or rock fragments, mere scratches. The guerrillas were running rampant, killing Japanese.

Inside the camp, the minutes before 0700hrs were the same as the opening of any other dreary day. The off-duty guards were forming up for calisthenics in loincloths, their rifles in the arms room. The next guard shift was armed, preparing to relieve the nightshift. The inmates were assembling for another boring roll call, cooks were preparing breakfast, and many of the nuns were completing their morning prayers.

When the nine transports rumbled over spewing out paratroopers, the relief guards ran back into their barracks while the calisthenics formation stood confused. Whoever was in charge made a mistake; he ordered them to run to their barracks and don uniforms before heading to the arms room. He probably judged that there would be time for this, not expecting the attack on the perimeter to begin immediately.

Lt Skau's team had beaten the guards to the arms room and was gunning them down. They shot down a Japanese officer diving through a window in the headquarters building. Unarmed guards were shot when found hiding in their barracks, outbuildings, ditches, and even internee barracks.

The internees still inside barracks hit the floor or crawled under cots when bullets began to snap through walls. Those outside flattened themselves on the ground, dove into ditches, or ran into barracks, which offered no cover. There were shouts and screams of both fear and joy as some immediately comprehended what was happening. When they saw the first parachutes others thought it was a food drop. Some inmates saw a P-38 wing over with RESCUE painted in yellow on its side. People shouted for family members, yelled advice on what to do, and nuns prayed with their rosaries. Some started collecting their possessions to move out. One woman saw soldiers trying to get through the perimeter wire, and running out tossed them a wire-cutter.

Running Japanese were dropping from fire coming both from within and from outside the camp. The unarmed loincloth-wearing guards scattered, trying to hide in barracks, ditches, and vegetation. Others fled outside the camp to be shot or macheted. Filipinos were reaping a grim revenge, and this would in turn result in an even more bloodthirsty lust for revenge. Some Japanese did make good their escape.

OVERLEAF

0700 HOURS, FEBRUARY 23, 1945 – H-HOUR
Sgt Cliff Town of the Provisional Reconnaissance Platoon and his small team of scouts and guerrillas struggled through the dense vegetation after crossing Boot Creek. As they approached their assigned position near the southwest corner of the Los Baños internment camp, firing broke out on the camp's far side. It quickly spread around its perimeter, even though not all of the assault teams were in position. The team's automatic rifleman, Pfc Robert Carroll, spotted four Japanese guards running from the camp across an open field. He emptied his M1918A2 BAR's 20-round magazine in one burst, downing them all. To reduce the BAR's weight and bulk, the flash suppressor and bipod had been removed. Another guard found crawling through a ditch was shot and then the team cut its way into the camp. By then most of the guerrillas had disappeared to hunt down fleeing Japanese.

While the camp was turning into a killing ground, the paratroopers were landing, shucking off harnesses, collecting weapons bundles, and rushing toward the camp. In contrast to many past combat jumps they landed close together right on the intended DZ. The well-marked, easily identifiable DZ, perfect weather, and low altitude all contributed to this. In spite of gullies, trees, fences, and the power line, there were no injuries and apparently no ground fire, although some jumpers claim that there was; they may have heard fire in the camp. Some jump injuries are almost inevitable on rough terrain with rapidly descending parachutes, and heavy equipment loads, but Company B was spared. Even the Filipinos making their first jumps were unscathed. One paratrooper did suffer a minor leg injury, but it did not stop him charging to the camp and doing his job. It was only afterwards when boarding an amtrac that he stiffened up.

The paratroopers were charging into the camp 15–20 minutes after the attack was launched, entering through openings cut by the scouts. The trip through the densely vegetated ravine leading to the camp had been difficult. Some had to overcome resistance on the perimeter. For the most part, the fighting was over other than mopping up holdouts and stragglers who had not yet fled. Inside the camp there was a great deal of confusion and the Americans were restricting their fire as over 2,100 internees ran about. The camp was far from secure. Japanese kept appearing all over, mostly trying to escape. The hardened veterans of Leyte and Manila were there to protect and rescue helpless civilians. They took no chances by sparing the enemy.

The engineer squad jumping in found their heavy demolition bundles and assembled in less than ten minutes. They sprinted off to establish their two roadblocks. The main one was 200 yards from the main gate. They blew down trees to create an abatis across Pili Lane, laid mines, and rigged command-detonated satchel charges. Two machine-guns covered the obstacles.

Guided by scouts picked up at the landing beach, Maj Burgess with the amtracs pressed on toward the camp. The Japanese on Mayondon Point fired on the amtracs, but with no effect. The amtracs reached the national highway, then rolled on to the camp.

They drove past Baker Memorial Hall and reaching the camp's main gate they saw a few guerrillas firing wildly. The pillbox beside the gate was knocked out and the gate partly open. The lead amtrac with Burgess and the amtrac battalion commander, LtCol Gibbs, crashed through. The remainder of Company A, 50 men, dismounted from the amtracs and secured the camp's sprawling interior as best they could. On hearing the amtracs' approach some inmates thought they were Japanese tanks.

Company C dismounted upon reaching the camp and established two roadblocks to the east with the assistance of the engineer platoon. They were to halt any enemy advance guard, fight a delaying action, and avoid casualties as much as possible.

Once the lead amtracs were inside, it was realized that there was no room for more than six. The narrow camp streets were soon grid-locked. The vehicles could not turn around and there were fears of running over internees who were scampering helter-skelter. The other amtracs were directed onto

the baseball field and other open areas outside the main gate. They lined up and dropped their tailgates. Two amtracs had broken down on the road.

Much to the surprise of many, out of one of the amtracs walked Col Courtney Whitney Sr,[15] the director of the classified Philippine Regional Section, the department of MacArthur's staff responsible for coordinating and supporting Philippine guerrilla organizations. He played no role in the command of the operation; he was merely an "observer." He and a civilian, probably an interpreter, and two amtrac crewmen entered the camp and returned with boxes of documents, believed to have been taken from the Japanese headquarters. The two returned to Mamatid on the first amtrac lift and to this day the boxes' contents are unknown.

Troops exit from the rear ramp of an LVT(4) amtrac. The vehicle could carry 24 men equipped for combat. Up to 35 liberated internees were jammed in along with their luggage during the exfiltration.

Success and evacuation

The inmates' emotions varied. Many were giddy with joy, but others were frightened and disoriented. Some ran and hid. Others calmly walked to the barracks and began collecting their meager possessions. They possessed little and what they had were often mementos from their pre-war lives. They had had to fight to hang on to them, with many valued items being sold or bartered for food. Thievery between inmates had been common. They were reluctant to leave these valuables behind, even if just worn-out clothes. Some prepared to depart, others thought that they had been liberated by advancing American forces and that there was no reason for immediate departure.

To the suddenly liberated inmates, interned for three years, their rescuers proved to be a shock. Seeing the American soldiers first from a distance, some thought they were Germans or even Japanese. They wore strange helmets more like a German helmet than the World War I "dishpan" helmets

---

15 Some references state that Whitney was a major general, but that was his rank when he resigned in 1951 after MacArthur's relief.

A view of the ravine leading from the drop zone to the northeast side of Los Baños camp. This proved to be a difficult route for the paratroopers as they made all haste to the camp. This modern photograph gives an idea of the density of the vegetation throughout the area. (Courtesy of David L. Robbins)

they had last seen American soldiers wearing. Those defenders of the Philippines had also worn khaki uniforms and carried bolt-action rifles. The rescuers wore dark green fatigues – the Japanese likewise had dark green uniforms – and had yellow skin, caused by atabrine anti-malaria medication. Their weapons too were strange; their M1 rifles, M1 carbines, M3 submachine guns, and bazookas were new to the internees. The amtracs were equally unfamiliar, massively larger than any tank they had seen. They were later in for a bigger surprise with regard to the amtracs.

Most startling to the internees was the "massive" size of their rescuers. To the liberated inmates, the well-fed and physically fit paratroopers looked huge. The average adult male internee was 110lb. The liberators themselves were shocked at the frail inmates who appeared to be nothing but skin and bones. They were even afraid to lift those unable to walk for fear of breaking them. After three years of seeing themselves waste away and seeing only small-statured Japanese and Filipinos, to the inmates' eyes average-sized fit Americans were giants.

To the liberators the freed men, women, and children were walking skeletons. They were dressed in ill-fitting rags, threadbare patched clothes, and homemade sandals with wooden soles. They walked slowly, many simply staggering, and could barely carry their few possessions. Many were suffering from malnutrition disorders, beriberi, malaria, tuberculosis, and other illnesses. The excitement was too much for some to bear and they cried, shouted incoherently, became euphoric, hid, or resisted cooperation. Some inmates ran to the kitchens and shoveled down food, while others raided Japanese storerooms. Food was more important than freedom for the moment. Sympathetic paratroopers and amtrac crewmen were giving them their D-ration chocolate bars, items from 10-in-1 rations stashed in the amtracs, and cigarettes. It was too rich for most and they were soon throwing up or at least sick in the stomach. Some internees were disappointed to learn that their rescuers were 'only' soldiers. They had in their minds that they would be liberated by marines.

Burgess realized that few of the internees were capable of walking 2½ miles to the San Antonio beach. Meanwhile he had other concerns. There was still sporadic firing around the area; he had no idea of the extent of paratrooper, scout, and guerrilla casualties or where the various elements were, and no reports on Japanese movements in the area. At the moment it seemed impossible to organize the internees, who were milling about and heading off in all directions. No one was in charge. At 0745hrs Skau reported to Burgess that all his men were accounted for, but many of the guerrillas had disappeared, apparently hunting Japanese. It was obvious that if a Japanese counterattack materialized, few guerrillas were under his control and able to assist effectively. Ringler reported that most of his paratroopers were accounted for, but that they too were having trouble organizing the internees. There were no bullhorns to direct them and no attempt was made to use the camp's public address system. Burgess could not establish radio contact with the Soule TF nor was there contact with the division. The Soule and Los Baños TFs were conducting their portions of the operation without any coordination between them. The firing heard from the west in the direction of the Soule TF was not advancing any closer. There were only two hours left before the three-hour deadline to remain in the camp. Burgess also realized that the camp itself was difficult to defend, as it was dominated by high ground. There were approaches on all sides offering cover and concealment. His force was too small to defend the entire perimeter and protect the internees. If he was hit by a heavy attack, with the Japanese enveloping the position as was their practice, he knew it would be impossible to escape with 2,100 panicked and unorganized civilians. It would be a massacre. LtCol Gibbs requested to be released to return to Mamatid, expecting the paratroopers and internees to link up with the Soule TF overland. That would be impossible.

FEBRUARY 23 1945

0700hrs H-Hour. Paratroopers begin descent & reconnaissance teams open fire on the camp

02/22/2008

Boot Creek ran around the south and southwest side of the internment camp. It proved to be an obstacle to the Reconnaissance Platoon scouts and guerrillas who positioned themselves around the camp to eliminate guard posts. (Courtesy of David L. Robbins)

The burning barracks of the camp. The amtracs are assembled in the open field in the foreground. The YMCA building, outside the camp, can be seen on the right center edge. 3,576ft high Mount Makiling rises in the background.

Burgess could not risk waiting for the Soule TF, especially since he was not in radio contact and had no idea if it was advancing, stalled, or withdrawing. His only option was to move everyone to the beach and evacuate by amtrac. There was one problem: the 54 amtracs could not carry all of the internees and soldiers in one lift. They would have to carry out as many internees as possible while his troops established a beach perimeter to protect the remaining civilians. It would be up to three hours before the amtracs returned. This presented a dilemma. The beach was on terrain that was difficult to defend, though at least he did not have to defend a 360-degree perimeter; they would be trapped with their backs to the water. Dense concealing vegetation surrounded it and it was dominated by the twin hills of Mayondon Point (230 and 180ft) a mile to the east. They were good on ammunition, had two howitzers, mortars, machine-guns, and bazookas. There were no known Japanese tanks in the area. However they were not in radio contact with the aircraft covering them and had no means to direct the fighter-bombers against threats.

Burgess knew it was imperative to get the internees organized and moving to the beach. As many as possible would ride in the amtracs. There were 130 who had to be carried into the amtracs on litters. The soldiers and the more fit internees would walk.

When Ringler reported to Burgess, he noted that the burning guard barracks was igniting adjacent buildings and that the blaze was moving toward the amtracs parked near the camp headquarters. Skau's firefight there had started the fire. The internees were drifting away from the fire towards the vehicles. It is reported that Burgess directed Ringler to fire the internee barracks, and that Ringler and Hattliner, the LMG platoon leader, did this themselves. They moved to the upwind side of the camp, the south side, and fired the barracks.

With the barracks burning and the flames spreading, the inmates began moving toward the amtracs on the baseball field. They were grabbing what possessions they could, but some were so weak they had to abandon them. The paratroopers were urging and directing them, trying to be as courteous

as they could. They understood fully what these people had endured, that they were in terrible condition, and that many were disoriented. Several panicky and confused inmates had to be more forcefully encouraged. One group of older gentlemen refused to leave unless they could take their considerable hoard of trunks and boxes. They were finally convinced when the barracks was fired. Former internees recalled soldiers acting like church ushers, cracking jokes, encouraging, helping where they could, but instilling a sense of urgency. Some soldiers were helping carry the baggage and even retrieving what had been dropped. They were carrying particularly weak inmates, children, and babies in their arms. One baby had been born three days before the raid. Suitcases and bags were being piled into amtracs and the civilians were climbing on top of them. The order was put out that ill internees, women, and children would be loaded onto the amtracs first.

Amtracs line up on the camp's entrance road, being unable to enter due to traffic congestion. Baker Hall is in the foreground.

This photo taken from a C-47 shows some of the barracks already smoldering. The light-colored building in the upper right is Baker Hall.

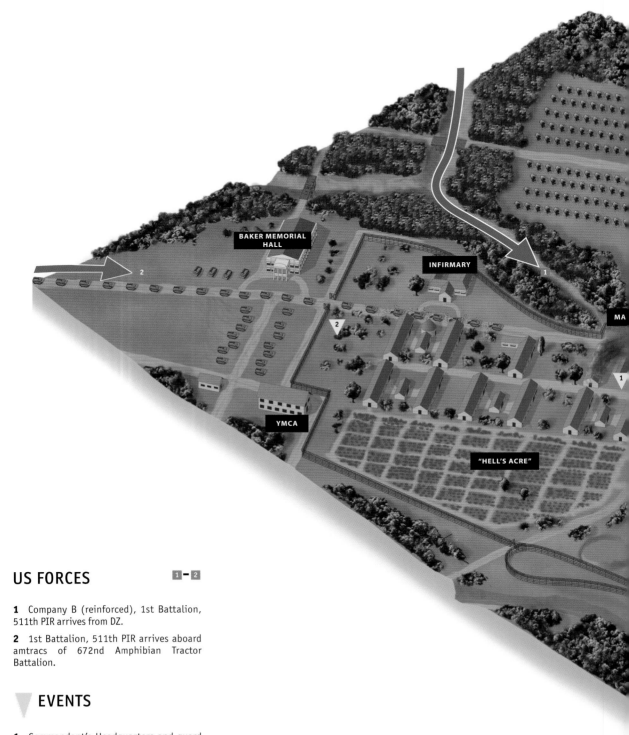

BAKER MEMORIAL
HALL

INFIRMARY

MA

YMCA

"HELL'S ACRE"

US FORCES

1 Company B (reinforced), 1st Battalion, 511th PIR arrives from DZ.

2 1st Battalion, 511th PIR arrives aboard amtracs of 672nd Amphibian Tractor Battalion.

EVENTS

1 Commandant's Headquarters and guard barracks ablaze.

2 Amtracs and internee assembly area.

EVACUATION COMMENCES

0715–0745 HOURS, FEBRUARY 23, 1945

Having struggled through the undergrowth on their route from the DZ, the men of Company B, 1st Battalion, 511th PIR arrived at the camp around 0715 hours, and immediately set about establishing a defensive perimeter, setting up roadblocks on the track leading to the camp's main gate. Shortly after, the amphibious task force, composed of men from the 1st Battalion, 511th PIR, deployed in amtracs of the 672nd Amphibian Tractor Battalion, made their way past the Baker Memorial Hall and into the camp where they set about rounding up and evacuating the internees.

"HOLY CITY"

Some 130 internees had to be carried to the amtracs on litters. Fortunately, over 200 litters had been brought along by the rescue party.

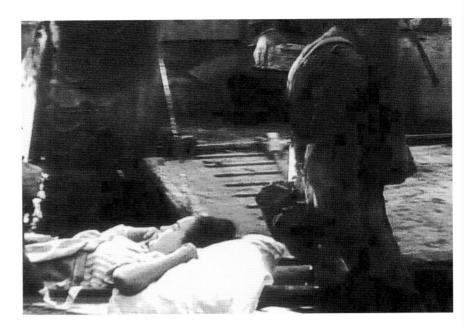

There were many men, especially older ones, who were in worse condition than some of the women. Husbands refused to be separated from their families and young men from their girlfriends, a reasonable demand under the circumstances.

What little fighting was ongoing was in the camp's southwest portion, the "Holy City" area. Missionaries, priests, and nuns were trying to clear out, but some were taking their time. Soldiers were fanning out through the camp, not only calling for everyone to clear out, but searching for hiding and lost inmates. They did not want to leave anyone behind. The able-bodied internees were already moving down the road, many carrying their baggage rather than risk losing it in amtracs. The first amtracs started out with

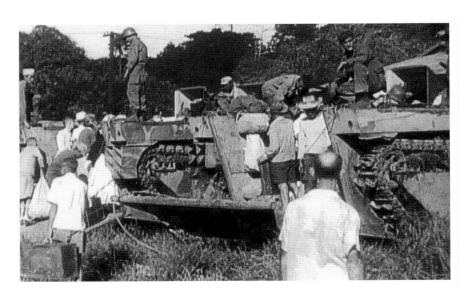

Liberated internees begin to load into the amtracs for transportation to San Antonio beach. The .50-caliber machine-gun shields are evident.

paratroopers walking alongside. Some walking internees made it only a short distance and had to be loaded aboard amtracs. A wonderful reunion was experienced by a United Press correspondent who had accompanied the amtracs. He located his interned brother and sister almost immediately after entering the camp.

An hour and a half after the raid had commenced, a small degree of order was being achieved. There were still too many lagging inmates and those loading were bringing too much baggage. When the first amtracs departed some inmates panicked and started to rush aboard others in fear of being left behind. By now all Company B paratroopers were accounted for. Burgess knew now that that he had suffered only two lightly wounded along with one internee. A very small number of internees had suffered minor injuries. Two Hunters ROTC guerrillas (Tana Castillo and Momong Soler) were killed and four wounded. Guerrillas were fast disappearing. Some were looting what they could from barracks. There would be virtually none to help defend the evacuation column or the beach.

With as many prisoners loaded as possible, the amtracs were filing onto Pili Lane heading for the beach. Up to 35 people were crammed into each. The two broken-down amtracs were now operational. Once the freed inmates were moving, most settled down and were enjoying the ride, waving at trudging Company A and C paratroopers escorting them. Further from the camp, jubilant Filipinos lined the road handing bananas and water up to the liberated internees. Some felt that they too had been liberated; the Americans were here and the Japanese were gone. Unfortunately that was not to be the case.

By 1130hrs the camp was cleared and most of it was in flames. Burgess and Ringler with Company B and the Reconnaissance Platoon made a final sweep and fell in behind the rumbling amtrac column as a rear guard. They assisted struggling civilians and carried babies and children. Japanese bodies

Obviously there was no threat as the civilians were loaded. Crewmen stood atop their amtracs directing civilians into unfilled vehicles.

Paratroopers and internees watch the barracks burn. Some internees, failing to understand the urgency of the situation, complained that their possessions were going up in smoke.

**FEBRUARY 23
1945**

**1000hrs
Lead amtracs
arrive at the
exfiltration point**

A barracks fully enveloped in flames. The fires were started by paratroopers in order to drive out the internees. It was difficult to convince them that they had to depart immediately.

dotted the road. The last element out of the camp was 2nd Platoon, Company B following at 15 minutes.

Soule Task Force actions

The glider troops were dug in and prepared to launch their attack down the highway toward the twin Lechería Hills at H-Hour. Just before 0700hrs they could see the transports winging across the lake and the white parachutes blossoming. The two artillery battalions opened fire on the hills and the Japanese position in the farther rock quarry. The infantry crossed the line of departure on the deep gorge of the San Juan River making a great deal of noise. The tank destroyers were kept moving about to make tank noises.

Priests and missionaries await evacuation across Laguna de Bay.

Trucks behind the lines dragged logs behind them to raise dust. The idea was to make the one-battalion attack appear to be a major offensive thrusting southeast. The goal was to attract 8th Division units in their direction, the supposed main attack, and away from Los Baños.

While enemy resistance was light, progress was slow, with bridges and culverts having to be repaired or bypassed. Col Soule was taking pains to minimize casualties. The clearance of the forested Lechería Hills, only about 200ft higher than the surrounding ground, was thorough. Soule wanted to ensure an unhindered withdrawal with the expected convoy of liberated internees. He still assumed his force would be linking up with the Los Baños TF. 1/188th GIR also supported the guerrilla attack on Calamba with mortars and long-range machine-gun fire. Filipino bodies were found with their hands tied. They may have been victims of the *Makapili* or *Makapili* executed by the guerrillas.

FEBRUARY 23 1945

c.1300hrs Amtracs begin returning

The lead amtracs begin moving out for San Antonio beach.

The advance continued slowly down the highway. Regardless of pains to limit casualties, two men in Company B were killed, as was the tank destroyer company commander. The area was not secured until after late morning, and as they pushed on the first amtracs were seen returning across the lake. From the Lechería Hills they could also make out artillery and mortar explosions in the Los Baños area. The Dampalit River rock quarry was reached at noon.

Based on what Soule could see, he determined that the Los Baños TF would not be linking up with him on the highway. He ordered a withdrawal back to the San Juan River. A battalion headquarters company soldier was hit during the withdrawal and died the next day. The final significant engagement was by Company A, when some 50 Japanese counterattacked and were repulsed. Soule would maintain a bridgehead on the enemy side in the event that he still had to move toward Los Baños.

Withdrawal

The amtracs, more than 2,100 joyous civilians, the Reconnaissance Platoon, and the battalion of paratroopers closed on San Antonio beach with some guerrillas still following. They immediately set about establishing a defense. The two howitzers were set up further inland. Burgess was still uncertain whether Soule TF was heading toward him. He thought he was still to march up the highway and meet them. Considering the insufficient space aboard the amtracs, some civilians would have to walk, as would all of the troops, burdened with weapons and ammunition. He had no idea if the enemy at the rock quarry and Lechería Hills had been neutralized nor if 8th Division forces were closing in.

The head of the column arrived at the beach at 1000hrs. With all amtracs and troops closed on the beach, Burgess made the decision to load as many of the civilians as possible – 1,500 – aboard and dispatch them to Mamatid with all haste. Some Company B troops accompanied them for protection. Orbiting P-38s watched over the amtracs. The remaining civilians and their stacked baggage would await the amtracs' return. This would require a

Some liberated internees were left on the beach with most of the paratroopers as 1,500 civilians were transported across the lake to Mamatid and safety.

On the San Antonio beach one of the first LVT(4) amtracs departs for Mamatid, loaded with liberated and joyous internees.

round trip of over two hours, so would be no earlier than 1300hrs, and the Japanese could attack the precarious beachhead at any moment. At least with their 75-mile range at sea they did not require time-consuming refueling before returning. Since departing Mamatid they had traveled only 7 miles by water and 5 by land.

The amtracs lined up in three columns of 18 and much to the surprise of the civilians simply drove into the water. They had no idea these massive vehicles could float. The crews aimed their machine-guns at the shore and cautioned their passengers to stay down. Occasional shots rang from the shoreline and they responded indifferently with casual return bursts. One group of six amtracs suppressed fire from Mayondon Point by driving along the shore peppering it with fire. They finally churned out into the lake. Two amtracs were hit by fire, causing the side flotation sponsons to flood. The passengers and their baggage were transferred to others and the two damaged amtracs towed home. A priest and the jump-injured paratrooper were swept off the bow of an amtrac when it crossed a sandbar. Another soldier dove in to support the injured paratrooper and the amtrac returned to recover all three.

The rear guard and last walking civilians reached the beachhead just before noon. Companies A and C had pulled back from their blocking positions and were establishing the perimeter. The Company C commander

On the beach at Mamatid the liberated internees off-load from amtracs, which then went back to retrieve the remaining internees along with the paratroopers defending them. Eighteen ambulances were on hand to transport the disabled to Muntinlupa.

reported that he had had some brushes with Japanese. Burgess was still in the dark about the status of Soule TF.

At noon a forward observer for the howitzers received a radio contact from Gen Swing, who was overhead in an L-4 Cub liaison aircraft. The forward observer put Burgess on the air with the general. Burgess reported his situation and what was underway; he expected that the amtracs were already on the way back to him. Swing was ecstatic that there were only minimal casualties and that the mission was so far successful.

Then Swing hit Burgess with a startling proposal. Swing suggested that once the final internees had departed in the returning amtracs, Burgess should secure Los Baños town and press west to link up with the Soule TF and limit his casualties. Burgess was stunned. He had fewer than 450 troops and a few dozen guerrillas. He would have no artillery support other than his two jeep-towed seventy-fives and mortars with limited ammunition, and no way to control air strikes. Not being in radio contact with Soule TF, he could not count on its artillery. The returning amtracs could not remain with Burgess as the XIV Corps commander had ordered their return for other missions. It was at least 7 road miles to the San Juan River and the Soule TF. They had no maps or aerial photos of the area. Other than medics they had no aid station, ambulances, or litters. They could be attacked on the move and in the open at any time. By now the 8th Division must be reacting and possibly advancing toward him and/or blocking the route west. If his force departed the beachhead by 1400hrs they had only four hours until sunset. Moving at night would be suicide and spending a 13-hour night and then attempting to move out in the morning would be equally dangerous. Although his men were in good condition and morale had peaked, they were tiring and had given their rations to civilians.

Burgess violated every principle of command and control. He turned off the radio, breaking his one communications link with higher headquarters. To have gone back on the air might well have resulted in Swing's ordering

Former internees loaded in a 2½ton cargo truck depart for Muntinlupa 15 miles to the north. It is difficult to imagine the sense of euphoria they must have felt.

him to take this exceedingly dangerous course of action, one not in his original mission. Most who have assessed his decision agree that he did the right thing. Fortunately for him, Swing was a very understanding and practical commander.

The amtracs began returning just after 1300hrs and the civilians boarded as the perimeter troops pulled in. The two howitzers were not informed of the withdrawal and had to rush to the beach. By the time they arrived many of the infantry had already departed. Japanese fire from the point was getting heavier and they dug in to await more amtracs. They loaded their guns and jeeps onto separate amtracs. One of the guns was manhandled in atop a pile of baggage. As it waded into the water, the crew fired a round back at the point and the recoil almost swamped the vehicle. The unhappy driver threatened to shoot them if they reloaded.

Internees are unloaded at Muntinlupa from some of the 21 GMC 2½ton cargo trucks that were on-hand to transport the civilians.

Japanese mortar and artillery rounds were falling and small-arms fire increased. The artillery was coming from the vicinity of the rock quarry. The last six amtracs with Burgess and Ringler went into the water at 1500hrs. One was almost hit by a mortar round and gave a civilian a slight head wound; another was grazed by a bullet and an amtrac crewman was slightly wounded. The fire was intense enough to cause the drivers to make frequent course changes as they fled. There was no estimate of how many Japanese were closing in. Left on the beach were some baggage and the remaining guerrillas reinforcing the beachhead defense. They melted into the forest. A few guerrillas had decided to go out with the amtracs.

The return

At Mamatid the civilians who arrived first had to wait an hour for transportation. They were all wandering about looking for friends and family, embracing every soldier they encountered, talking of their adventure, and unloading baggage. This last they were urged to accomplish quickly; the amtracs needed to be on their way. The 11th Abn Div had assembled 21 2½-ton trucks and 18 ambulances to shuttle them 15 miles north to

¾ton Fargo Motor Corp. ambulances arrive at New Bilibid prison. They could carry four litter patients.

Muntinlupa. There they were greeted by cheering soldiers and Filipinos. Unloading inside the walls of New Bilibid prison, they were surprised to be quartered in cells. It was a safe place, though, and the doors remained open. Medical personnel examined everyone, clothes were passed out, and hot bean soup and fresh bread and butter – to be easy on their distended stomachs – were abundant. Some returnees went through the chow line four times. War correspondents shot film and photos, and interviewed the returnees. There was a distinctly festive air. The trucks and ambulances plied back and forth throughout the day to bring the Americans, British, Dutch, Canadians, Australians, Poles, Italians, and Norwegians to their temporary home. The last group arrived at 1600hrs. Rosters were compiled and families reunited. XIV Corps took charge of the returnees, relieving the 11th Abn Div of their responsibility. The returnees were euphoric about their deliverance and well fed; surprisingly only 107 had to be hospitalized because of malnutrition, illness, or, in three cases, pregnancy. Gradually they were processed and temporary residences were found; the last were gone by 8 March. Some began arriving back in the United States in May, but many stayed in the Philippines.

The last of the liberating paratroopers arrived at 1700hrs and the returnees applauded and cheered themselves hoarse. Granted, they had simply done their job, but they had made every effort to safeguard the internees, were overwhelmingly courteous and helpful in the heat of battle, and had gone out of their way to see to the prisoners' comfort, even giving up their rations and water. They spent the night at the prison eating and rejoicing with the returnees. An hour after breakfast the regimental commander ordered the battalion to load up; they had a war to win.

Chow lines were in readiness for the half-starved civilians. They were served all the bean soup and hot bread and butter they wanted.

ANALYSIS

As his battalion marched up the highway, Burgess was summoned to the division headquarters for a press conference. There he found that higher staff officers were taking credit for the mission's planning and development. The plan had been developed solely by the division and his own staff. A written operation order had not even been published. To clarify who was responsible Col Quandt, the division G-3, and Burgess sat down, wrote the operation order (OPORD) using hindsight, and saw it distributed to higher headquarters. XIV Corps and Sixth Army then copied the orders and

Eleven US Navy nurses were held at Los Baños and rescued with the internees. They were the only US military personnel in the camp. Chief Nurse Laura Cobb tells Vice Admiral Thomas C. Kinkaid, commanding Seventh Fleet, of their experiences.

backdated them. Unfortunately, this set of OPORDs has been used as an example of how well subordinate units executed higher headquarters' orders, when in fact the higher headquarters had never issued the example orders.

There is no doubt that this was an effectively executed operation in spite of the complexity of delivering forces by vastly different means at precisely the correct time. Simply marshalling and coordinating the delivery assets and the units was extremely challenging. The relatively smooth movement of the many moving pieces – Reconnaissance Platoon, different guerrilla forces, parachute company, the rest of the parachute battalion and its attachments, the several units of the diversionary force, the amtrac battalion, and the C-47 flight as well as supporting air cover – could only have been accomplished by well-trained, experienced, and flexible leaders. This is even more fully demonstrated by the fact that the operation commander, LtCol Soule, never had radio contact with the Los Baños TF, as a result of which Maj Burgess was in sole command at Los Baños.

A great deal of imagination was shown, especially in regard to the use of the amtracs' unique capabilities to deliver the follow-on parachute battalion and to evacuate the internees and troops. This was totally unexpected by the Japanese. The delivery of a company by parachute immediately adjacent to the camp was excellent. It provided a major distraction for Japanese units in the area, and, along with the simultaneous attack by the diversionary force from the west and the landing of 54 amtracs, reinforced the impression that a major offensive was underway. It no doubt added to the confusion of the Japanese guards that upon seeing the paratroopers they were struck by an immediate ground attack, whereas they might have expected to have some time before the paratroopers assembled, made their way to camp, and then attacked. Indeed the speedy arrival of the paratroopers on the heels of the scout and guerrilla attack served several purposes. It reinforced the Japanese confusion; backed up the somewhat piecemeal initial attack on the camp; quickly provided manpower to more rapidly secure the camp, establish its

The New Bilibid prison at Muntinlupa, as seen today, was the new home for the liberated internees. They were at first surprised by their accommodations, but the prison had been cleaned out, the doors left open, and food and medical care made available. (Courtesy of David L. Robbins)

defense, and help organize the internees; and would have provided a valuable reinforcement if the guards had been able to establish organized resistance.

There were problems, as there always are. The reliance on paddle- and wind-powered *bancas* to deliver the Reconnaissance Platoon was risky. This could have prevented them being in position on time. As it was some of the teams were late in arriving, mainly because of the rough terrain, dark night, and sometimes less than knowledgeable guides. If they had arrived even a few minutes later, the Japanese might have reacted more strongly. While the guerrillas played an important role, they were not always as reliable and disciplined as might have been necessary. Many went after the Japanese, looted, or simply left the area rather than organize themselves into a viable defense and escort force. There were, however, others who did continue to assist the Americans throughout the operation. Their overall aid in collecting and relaying intelligence, assisting the rescuers, and otherwise participating was invaluable. It would have been a much more difficult operation to execute without their aid and would have required a larger US force. It is estimated that up to 800 guerrillas participated in different capacities.

There was apparent confusion as to how the internees were to be evacuated: by amtrac, by moving toward the Soule TF for pick-up, or by awaiting the Soule TF. While the flexibility to employ any of these options should have been maintained, a single main course of action should have been planned, namely the amtrac evacuation. Of course this confusion could have been alleviated if the Soule and Los Baños TFs had been in radio contact. The fact that the Soule TF callsigns and frequencies were never delivered to the Los Baños TF was a major failing and could have led to a dangerous situation. It is a mystery why more effort was not made to get that information to Burgess. It could have been dropped by liaison aircraft once the amtracs were ashore. It may well be that the division was unaware that the courier had never delivered it to Burgess before he departed. As it was, the two task forces were not aware of each other's situation or subsequent plans, and Burgess could not request artillery support from Soule as his artillery moved forward. If the Japanese had mounted a major counterattack it could have been disastrous. Another problem was that no air control party was present to direct fighter support.

Fortunately, the Japanese response was sluggish, unorganized, and piecemeal. It must have appeared that a major offensive was underway and they chose to hold their positions to face an attack. They did not react in a manner appropriate to pursuing a withdrawing rescue force. An estimated 70–80 of the guards were killed. There are no official estimates of losses inflicted by the Soule TF, air strikes, and artillery: possibly 100–200.

Overall, the Los Baños raid was a superbly planned and executed operation with the leaders demonstrating a great deal of flexibility and effective on-the-spot decision making. Many accounts dwell on the mission's "high risk" and "long shot odds." The commanders insist that it was not as risky as it is made out to be. Gen Swing and Maj Burgess maintained that it was just another operation and that nothing about it was special. Perhaps not, but the leaders and men were special indeed.

CONCLUSION

The 1/511th PIR was marched 10 miles south to occupy the San Juan River positions previously occupied by Soule TF, which had returned to Manila. Since the Japanese had been stirred up, it was felt necessary to contain them. Burgess considered that the original positions were too exposed to the reoccupied Lechería Hills and established new positions on more defendable ground 600 yards to the rear. He booby-trapped the original positions and when the Japanese attacked that night they were shelled and mortared, leaving 40 dead.

After a week of American harassment, the Japanese withdrew to Los Baños with the paratroopers on their heels. What the Americans found horrified and angered them. Starting two nights after the raid, troops of the 17th Infantry Regiment and *Kempeitai* had commenced terror raids starting at the *barrios* (small villages) nearest the camp. They were backed by Filipino *Ganaps* – paramilitary units led by Japanese NCOs. Up to 1,500 Filipino civilians had been massacred over the following nights. Entire families were tied to the stilts of their off-the-ground homes and the structures burned. Seventy people hiding in a church were burned. Individuals were bayoneted and beheaded. A family of three Americans who had not been interned was murdered. It was nothing more than revenge for the assistance provided to the raiders by local guerrillas. Guerrillas attempted to intervene, but were no match for the well-armed Japanese. The guerrillas had also urged civilians to flee, but most ignored the warning. Warrant Officer Sadaaki Konishi, the much-hated internee tormentor, had escaped and was involved in the atrocities directed by Col Fujishige commanding the 17th Infantry. Chinese too in the area were murdered as they were considered pro-American. The slaughter spread to other towns in Laguna Province.

Konishi had escaped with seven guards and witnessed the slaughter of other guards by the guerrillas accompanying the Reconnaissance Platoon. He made his way to Mount Makiling and joined up with the Saito Battalion. Maj Iwanaka, the camp commandant, also escaped.

There is a great deal of controversy in regard to the post-raid reprisals. Many of the guerrilla leaders place the blame on US forces for failing to

secure the area. This was impossible with the forces available and the 11th Abn Div's and Sixth Army's need to first secure Manila before clearing southern Luzon. Certain guerrilla units were tasked with securing the area. It appears that some made no effort to do so. What remained was insufficient. Even if all available guerrilla resources had been employed and some degree of supply could have been effected by Sixth Army, it is doubtful whether they could have prevented the massacre. The 11th Abn Div had only three understrength battalions with limited support available, and two of these had to be returned to Manila. All three battalions could not have secured Laguna Province against the raging 8th Division. Frankly, the post-raid security of the area was inadequately addressed by all parties.

The inhabitants of *barrios* around Los Baños were to suffer from vicious Japanese reprisals for a week after the raid. The Japanese "reasoned" that the civilians in the area were guerrillas, relatives of guerrillas, or had in some way aided the guerrillas and Americans.

Postscript

In July 1945 a former internee was playing golf on the restored Los Baños course. By chance he spotted Warrant Officer Sadaaki Konishi in a POW work detail. Konishi was charged with intentionally starving internees and on several counts of ordering troops to murder American, Filipino, and Chinese civilians. He was tried in January 1947 and hanged in June.

In January 1948 Company B, 1st Battalion, 511th PIR and the Provisional Reconnaissance Platoon were awarded the Distinguished Unit Citation for their action at Los Baños. The degree of heroism required is the same as that warranting award of a Distinguished Service Cross to an individual, the second highest award for valor after the Medal of Honor. (This award was redesignated the Presidential Unit Citation in 1966.)

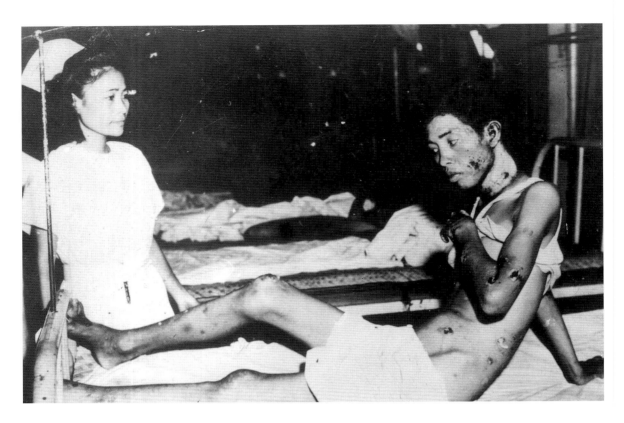

This Japanese atrocity victim had been bayoneted multiple times and survived the Anos church fire in which at least 70 victims perished. The church has since been rebuilt.

Unfortunately no dramatic motion picture of this spectacular operation has ever been made, but The History Channel produced a 100-minute documentary available on DVD, *Rescue at Dawn: The Los Baños Raid*. Released in 2004 it includes footage of the site today, reenactor recreations, surviving military and civilian participants, and vintage film and photos.

Nothing remains of the Los Baños internment camp today. The buildings were burnt during the raid; what remained, including the barbed wire fences, was removed by Japanese POWs and the golf course was reopened before the war was even over. The site is now occupied by the sprawling University of the Philippines at Los Baños, which was reestablished in 1949. The barracks area was restored as playing fields known as D. L. Umali Freedom Park. They are overlooked by a carillon bell tower and the renowned Fertility Tree, a massive rain tree where lovers frolic. Barker Memorial Hall again serves as a gymnasium.

One of the Los Baños inmates, Frank W. Buckles, today is 108 years old and the last surviving US veteran of World War I.

BIBLIOGRAPHY

Arthur, Anthony. *Deliverance at Los Baños*. New York: St. Martin's Press, 1985. (Main focus is the internees.)

Cogan, Frances B. *Captured: The Japanese Internment of American Civilians in the Philippines, 1941–1945*. Athens, GA: University of Georgia Press, 2000.

Flanagan, Edward M., Jr. *The Angels: A History of the 11th Airborne Division, 1943–1946*. Washington, D.C.: Infantry Journal Press, 1948.

Flanagan, Edward M., Jr. *The Angels: A History of the 11th Airborne Division*. Novato, CA: Presidio Press, 1989. (While a similar title, this is an entirely different book than the 1948 edition.)

Flanagan, Edward M., Jr. *The Los Baños Raid: The 11th Airborne Division Jumps at Dawn*. Novato, CA: Presidio Press, 1986. (Re-released 1999 as *Angels at Dawn: The Los Baños Raid*. Main focus is the military operation.)

Holland, R.B. *The Rescue of Santo Tomás, Manila, WWII – The Flying Column: 100 Miles to Freedom*. Nashville, TN: Turner Publishing, 2003.

Nash, Grace C. *That We Might Live: A Story of Human Triumph during World War II*. Scottsdale, AZ: Shano Publishers, 1984. (Re civilian internees at Los Baños.)

Robbins, David L. *Broken Jewel*. New York: Simon & Schuster, 2009. (A novel.)

Rottman, Gordon L. *World War II Pacific Island Guide: A Geo-Military Study*. Westport, CT: Greenwood Publishing, 2001.

Smith, Robert R. *US Army in World War II: Triumph in the Philippines*. Washington, D.C.: Center for Military History, 1963.

INDEX